How to Run Away from Home After 50

A True RV Adventure
by
Anita S. Henehan

ISBN 0-9727951-0-3

Design: Karen Saunders
Editing: Barbara McNichol
Cover Concept: Jim Schomaker
Cover Illustration: Fred Eyer
Printing: United Graphics, Inc.

Reflections Publishing
4218 Olive Street
St. Louis, MO 63108

Praise for
How to Run Away from Home After 50

Anita's depiction of life on the road grabs your attention and won't let go . . . definitely a must read.

— Pam Shelton, Manager of Casino Queen RV Park, East St. Louis, IL

A delightful adventure. I especially like Anita's honesty on how she felt while making such big changes in her life. I identified with many of them and it gives me courage that I, too, can "Run Away From Home" and have wonderful experiences.

— Peg Carter, new full-time RVer

Anita Henehan's book How To Run Away From Home After 50 *is a wonderful story that describes the requirements necessary for deciding to become a full-time RVer. I would recommend this great travelogue to anyone. Anita clearly outlines the do's and don'ts, the good times and the problem times as she and her husband travel around North America. Her accurate recommendations serve as a guide for anyone thinking about RVing . . . whether full-time or part-time.*

— Francis Montgomery,
Holiday Rambler, Clydesdale Rambler

Once I started reading it, I couldn't put it down. Just had to finish it fast.

— Eileen Shapiro

This book is a wonderful diary of a courageous change in lifestyle filled with marvelous descriptions and terrific hints, places to go, things to do.

— Esther Thaller

Anita, your fortitude and adventurous spirit have been marvelous. I learned a great deal from your book and I am sure others will also.

— Gary Shapiro

Entertaining and informative, How To Run Away From Home After 50 *is great reading for RVers, whether experienced or want-to-be's. The tips offered in the book of things to look out for and interesting places to visit are helpful.*

— Bud Morris, new full-time RVer

Anita, I enjoyed reading about your adventures in your Holiday Rambler Navigator. Your struggles to embrace the RV lifestyle should be very helpful for others contemplating the same change. Holiday Rambler has been serving folks like you for 50 years, promoting the lifestyle adventure and spirit of exploration your book so accurately portrays. We are proud to have you and your husband Paul as part of our family.

— Mike Spencer, National Sales Manager,
Holiday Rambler Motorized

Dedication

I dedicate this book to Linda Nash, my dear friend. Without Linda's encouragement, this book would have never happened.

An author, public speaker, and personal coach, Linda is a perfect example of bouncing back from all adversities. Be sure to read her latest book *The Bounce Back Quotient.* Thanks for everything, Linda, and mostly for having faith in me.

Book Cover

The idea for the cover of *How to Run Away from Home After 50* was developed by Jim Schomaker, a dear friend. With his wife Karen, we have shared wonderful experiences together. Thanks a million, Jim. I am grateful for your talents, efforts, and friendship. The cover was designed by Karen Saunders, and the cover illustration was done by Frederic Eyer.

Acknowledgments

I want to express my sincere thanks to my husband, Paul, my partner in this incredible journey. His love, help, and patience have encouraged me all along the way.

I also want to thank my niece and nephew Susan and Chris Coker whose efforts have helped me complete this book, and Barbara McNichol, who is the most fabulous, patient, persistent editor and person I have ever encountered. This book never could have become a reality without her knowledge and assistance.

Note from the Author

This book is a book of courage. I have had to find courage all my life to get through all the circumstances that have brought me to this time. After the accidental death of my first husband and suicide of my son, running away from home took a high degree of courage for a woman who'd lived in the same home almost all her life.

Since we took off in May, 2000, Paul, my second husband, has helped me turn this traveling adventure into an incredible journey. I could have never done it without him. And I'm happy to say we have never regretted running away!

As you read about our adventures, I hope *How to Run Away from Home After 50* also gives you courage to do whatever you wish. Follow your dreams. Life is short and every day is a gift.

— Anita Sokolik Henehan

How to Run Away from Home After 50

Introduction

It happened late afternoon on a Sunday in October 1999. A rear tire on our 25-foot trailer exploded just outside of Anchorage, Alaska. The tire blew so fast, we had no time to even pull off of the highway.

I immediately got out of the Chevy Tahoe and took off my purple sweatshirt. I started waving at the cars coming toward us. The drivers couldn't see that we were stopped until they got too close to our RV so they sailed on by. Luckily, I had my cell phone so I called information and told the operator about our dilemma. Paul took over the sweatshirt-waving while I called for help and got the numbers of gas stations nearby.

There was no way Paul and I could change the large, heavy tire on the RV by ourselves. As I started to make the calls, we worried that we might not be able to get help until the next day, which was a business day. We stayed there feeling helpless for what seemed like an eternity.

Then out of the blue, a driver stopped and got out of his car. We were suspicious of him at first, not knowing his intentions, until we saw he was wearing slippers. His friendly approach quickly put us at ease. He told us that flat tires often happen along this rugged highway, that he had experienced several himself and knew what we were going through. With kindness and energy, he helped Paul change the tire and we were on our way again. "People just help each other," he said with a generous smile.

That's precisely why I've written this book. Just as this kind traveler wearing slippers helped us, I hope this book gives you insights about traveling RV-style and leaving your old lifestyle behind.

For our first adventurous foray into RVing, we tested the idea on a three-month trip traveling from Missouri to Alaska. The adventures we had on that trip gave us much more than memories; it totally changed our lives. Here's another adventure.

*In Homer, Alaska, Paul and I parked our RV
right out on the spit surrounded by the waters of
Kachemak Bay so we could enjoy having the feel of
the ocean right next to us. After we got settled, we
wanted some exercise and asked people around us
for ideas on a good place to hike. "Up to the glacier,
which is across the bay," they told us. But the only
way to get across was to take a water taxi, so we
had to hunt for Maco, the owner of the only water
taxi there.*

*Maco chauffeured us across the bay in his boat,
then showed us where to begin hiking. He said he
would pick us up sometime that afternoon, that is,
if he didn't forget. It amused us when he said he
had left quite a few folks there and they had started
their own community. It sounded like he was
kidding, but then again we weren't absolutely sure.*

*After hiking up the trail for several miles, we
reached the glacier we had been told about.
What a spectacular place, well worth the three-
hour climb. We stopped and ate our picnic*

lunch, soaking in the beauty of this incredible glacier. Could this be really happening? Were we actually sitting next to a glacier? How different from our suburban home it was. How awesome.

Before long, we started our long trek back to the beach area where Maco said he would pick us up. In the meantime, it began raining and the steep terrain underfoot got extremely slippery. Luckily our walking sticks helped us reach the bottom of the trail safely.

After several hours of waiting on the beach, Maco and the water taxi finally showed up. Thank goodness we didn't have the join the community of people he had forgotten to pick up over the years.

Back in St. Louis, Missouri, Paul and I lived in a 3,000 square-foot house. I had actually resided here for 37 years—about nine of those with Paul, who is my second husband. I had spent almost four decades decorating and redecorating this home. After I remodeled one room, I'd lovingly renovate the next. Each room—even the bathrooms and the basement—had to have artwork plus accessories that matched perfectly.

In contrast, decorating becomes simple when living in an RV. Since it's already furnished, there are few opportunities to add personal touches. Believe me, trading a large home for a trailer takes a lot of getting used to.

I stock the RV with only a few clothes for hot as well as cool temperatures. We need a minimum number of kitchen items, but of course we restock the pantry often. Unfortunately, we can't stock the RV with the close friends we have known over the years. Along with enjoying the adventures of traveling to new places, we also had to come to terms with all of the people we were leaving behind.

Yet traveling in our RV—we call it Merrily We Roll Along—we've discovered we are welcome guests everywhere we go. RVing has expanded our ability to visit people all over. We've gotten in touch with family and friends we haven't seen in many years. I have been fortunate to meet Paul's family, spread out across the U.S., for the first time. We are also getting reacquainted with my relatives and friends on the east coast as well as the west coast.

I'd say RVing is a golden opportunity for us 50 year olds to be with people we care about yet rarely see. As we travel, we take our time and stop whenever we see a place of interest. When we feel tired, we stop to rest. When we get hungry, we have food in the refrigerator to eat. Traveling in an RV is so handy, easy, and fun. I love the flexibility it brings to our lives.

But my life hasn't always rolled along this smoothly. This story explains what I mean.

Over the years, my first husband Herb Sokolik and I raised three children. In 1979, we were in a tragic boating accident and Herb lost his life. At the time of the accident, Karen was 19, Steven was 18, and Roger was 15. We had a cottage at the river outside of St. Louis where we spent weekends relaxing and boating. Our boys especially loved to water ski behind our boat.

That summer, Herb was finally taking time off to spend with his family. He had been working hard operating two drugstores—a stressful time. One of the drugstores had been robbed and a pharmacist shot. Herb was exhausted from running the stores and going to the hospital to visit Ron, the injured pharmacist. We deeply needed to take a vacation and, since our place at the river was only one hour from home, we opted to go there for a few days of fun. Herb, our son Roger, Roger's friend Tom, and I left for a mini-vacation.

However, as soon as we got to where our boat was moored, we found out the motor wasn't running properly. So we took it in for repairs, asking the people at the repair shop to hurry and fix it because we only had a few days off. They complied with our wishes and quickly fixed the motor . . . or so we thought.

The next day, we decided to take the boat through the locks to Pere Marquette State Park . . . Roger had had a fight with his dad and decided not to go on the outing, so Herb, Tom, and I left for the day. As we were waiting to go through the locks at the Winfield Dam, the boat's motor died. We couldn't get it started again, but the boat kept moving forward toward the dam. We signaled for help, but no one noticed our distress.

As we got closer and closer to the dam abutment, I became paralyzed with fear. I started to get my life jacket on and Herb began putting on his ski belt when the boat struck the dam. Before I knew what was happening, I was thrown clear. Tom managed to jump out onto the abutment, but the boat got sucked under the dam and Herb was trapped inside.

When the Corp of Engineers arrived at the boat, it was too late. They found me floating in the river with the help of my life jacket. I had gone under the dam and had a big, knotted bruise on my head, but otherwise I was physically all right. So was Tom, who had safely reached shore. But Herb died instantly when the boat hit the dam—a severe blow to everyone.

Roger had never forgiven himself for not being with us the day of the accident. He believed he could have saved his dad. In fact, he felt so tormented about it, he committed suicide ten years later.

Because I had raised our children in this spacious house in St. Louis, my attachment to it was greater than ever. Roger was born in this house. He loved it and had always said he wanted to buy it from us when he grew up.

However, I have always loved to travel, even as a small child. My parents could never afford to go anywhere, but my aunt and uncle took me with them to Florida twice when I was a teenager. I can remember the minute details of those trips to this day. When Paul and I met, we quickly learned that traveling was a common passion and one that has served us both well.

On our inaugural trip to Alaska in 1999, we had spent three months relaxing and seeing this beautiful land. We had lived comfortably in our trailer without problem—just the perfect size to take to Alaska, we decided. Because of this trip, I realized I could live in a smaller space than I ever imagined. I didn't need a lot of stuff . . . and that was truly a revelation!

We had offered to baby-sit our two grand-children when we returned home to St. Louis from Alaska. Paul's son Paul and daughter-in-law Joan were relocating back to the U.S. from Lincoln, England. Joan and the children arrived shortly after our return and she needed time to shop for a house. Sam was three-and-a-half years old; his little sister Sophia was only ten-and-a-half months old. It had been a long time since we had taken care of little ones. We had wonderful times playing with them at the park every day. Yet it took both of us every minute of the day to keep the kids busy. Two full weeks later, after their parents picked them up, I went to bed exhausted.

As I was recovering, I had a conversation with God and asked Him what I should do to get back to a healthy, simple life and recuperate completely. God spoke to me in his own way. He told me I was strong enough to sell the house and that is what I should consider doing.

I realized that Paul and I needed to find a living situation that was uniquely ours, not part of my past. I felt we owed it to our wonderful relationship to have our own place. That belief strengthened my resolve. So I told Paul I wanted to sell my home of 37 years and travel full-time. He responded with shock and excitement. Though we both love traveling, he advised me to think carefully about this possibly outrageous decision. He said that once I made up my mind, there was no turning back.

We considered renting a small apartment to come home to—an emotional safety net—but decided it would be too costly for the amount of time we'd spend there. So we agreed to start off in our trailer and see how RVing full-time

would work. In the back of my mind, I knew we
could always buy another house if and when we
wanted to settle again.

This introduction gives you an idea what set us on the road to RV living. In the chapters that follow, I've compiled tips, ideas, and information we found valuable before we "ran away from home." I hope to save you some steps along the way so that you can "roll merrily along," too.

Chapter 1
Getting Started

Before we even considered buying an RV, we rented one for a week to test our "togetherness." But that was just the beginning; we had many decisions to make before we could "run away from home." This was our approach:

Step 1: Deciding what to do with our home.

    a. Do we want to sell?

    b. Do we want to rent it out?

    c. Do we want to maintain it?

Step 2: Put the house up for sale and downsize.

This was the best option for us though, for me, it was one of the most difficult things I had ever done. We also had to get rid of all the things we had stored in closets that we didn't wear, didn't use, and didn't need.

I had owned my piano since I was eight

years old. I remember begging to take piano

lessons and my parents surprising me by buying

me a piano. For sentimental reasons, I had a

hard time letting go of it. I did sell it for a reasonable price to a family whose children would enjoy using it.

Our breakfast room furniture had been custom made, designed by one of my favorite artists, Brother Mel Meyer, affiliated with the Marianist Gallery. This metal and glass table and chairs were a focal point of our kitchen, and we had become attached to the set. Luckily, one of our friends who admired the set offered to buy it. Now every time we travel back to our St. Louis neighborhood, we visit her and our breakfast room set. That made it easier for me to let go.

We had to decide what to give to our children. This included the china, crystal, and silverware. We shipped some paintings and other valued possessions to Florida and Colorado for them.

Little by little, we packed boxes and took them to the shed. It took me several months to emotionally release all the stuff I'd collected over the years. Every time I'd walk through the house, I'd remember where something came

from and feel nostalgic. Every decision
seemed heartbreaking.

I tried to keep in mind the excitement
of being free of "all this stuff." I vowed to
never lose sight of the Big Picture. After
all, it was only stuff. So I'd focus on the
adventures ahead—a whole new opportu-
nity to live life to its fullest. We resolved
that our new life would be unencumbered
by possessions and responsibilities.

Step 3: Get a storage locker.

Despite the downsizing, we still had items we simply couldn't part with or would use later, so we put
them in a storage locker!

Step 4: Work with professionals to sell possessions and home.

We hired a reputable estate sale expert Michael Lloyd
in St. Louis, who is affiliated with The Designing Block.
His firm takes care of everything, even arranging for
cleaning the house after it sold. We recommend Michael
very highly. We also chose a reputable realtor who over-
saw the sale of the house that took about four months.

We lived in the trailer in the driveway while our estate sale was being set up. As people went through the house, they asked, "What happened to the people? Did they die?" "No," Michael replied. "They are out back in their trailer." We amused many people by our new lifestyle. In fact, during the estate sale, some people even asked to buy the trailer. Sorry, Not For Sale.

As a way to say goodbye to 37 years in this home, I did some releasing ceremonies and wrote letters to my first husband with whom I had purchased it. I also wrote a letter to my son, Roger. The trees in the yard we had planted in his memory when he passed away were particularly hard to leave.

Finally, I wrote a letter to the house—saying what it had meant to all of us. Then I burned the letters in the fireplace and found peace in doing so.

As soon as I symbolically released the house through the letter-burning ritual, we got three contracts in one weekend! I prayed that the new owners would love and appreciate the house as we had. We got our wish.

As hard as it is, there is always light at the end of the tunnel.

Chapter 2
Moving Out

St. Charles, Missouri

With our home in St. Louis now sold, we moved into our trailer "Merrily We Roll Along," which was 25 feet long and pulled by our Chevy Tahoe. What a sight to see going down the road.

Sundermeier's Trailer Park in downtown St. Charles was our parking place for our first three weeks of RVing. Living there gave us a feeling of freedom. We chose to stay in St. Charles, which is close to St. Louis, so we could wrap up details of my business (an art dealership) and enjoy nice dinners with friends and family.

Staying in this location also offered some time for Paul to recover from surgery for two melanomas on his back. Three weeks after his operation, the doctor removed the second set of staples. Thank God, he was given a clean bill of health. That very day—May 23, 2000—we left St. Louis. It truly was the first day of the rest of our lives.

*Always, we kept the vision of an Exciting
Spiritual Journey. We felt grateful that God had
given us yet another opportunity to experience life
and live our dream. We believed that wherever we
would go from here would be pure paradise.
We were running away from home.*

Step 5: Take care of yourself on the road.

It is easy to neglect your health while on the road so I
schedule regular massages and chiropractic care and follow a
regular exercise program with walking, weights, and video-
tapes for stretching. There are many ways to take care of yourself AND there is nothing more important at home or on the
road. If you don't know where to go to get these services, go to
a local health food store. The people there provide a wealth of
information on all levels.

Tip: Health Care is a very important issue to get in order.
We made sure our health care insurance would cover us wherever we traveled. We use referral services that help us find
chiropractors in different states. However, we still have all of
our healthcare practitioners in St. Louis. So every six months,
we return to our home city to get dental check-ups and, every
fall, we go back for our annual physicals.

Step 6: Line up all insurance.

Make sure your health care insurance is paid up and in order.

Have your car and RV insurance paid up and in order.

Have all pertinent phone numbers and insurance cards handy. And take your medical records with you, especially if you have any medical problems that may need care as you travel.

Chapter 3
Purchasing Your RV

Seven years ago, we were planning our vacation. Since we had never been in an RV before, we rented one. After we were shown the mechanics of hooking up the water, electricity, and sewer, we brought it home to load for the week's journey.

It took us hours to put everything we might need in the trailer for a week: the clothing, the food and so on. After several hours and many trips from the house to the trailer, I sighed, "Who ever thought of this idea? It would be so much easier to go to a motel." When we finally finished about dinnertime, Paul said, "Let's wait until tomorrow to leave. I really don't want to drive and have to set up in the dark."

We left the next morning and drove about three hours to the Eminence, Missouri, area. It was September and the parks were empty, as the children had returned to school, making it even easier for us to enjoy the peacefulness and the beauty of the area. We had brought our bikes and enjoyed biking around the park as well as hiking.

After this truly relaxing week, Paul looked 10 years younger. I asked him, "Well, what do you think?" and he replied, "I think we are going to have to get an RV."

At that time, I owned a Toyota station wagon and Paul had a company car. We knew we would have to purchase a vehicle with a V8 engine to pull a travel trailer. We shopped around and liked the looks and convenience of the Chevy Tahoe. It would definitely fill all of our needs. Luckily, we found an almost-new demo with five thousand miles on it. I liked the maroon color and we bought it.

This all happened 24 hours after we decided to get a travel trailer. And not long after that, I sold my six-year old Toyota to the first person who looked at it.

Actually, we had no idea what kind or size of trailer to buy. We continued to look around and ask questions. We weren't in a hurry; it was fall and we wouldn't be using it until the next spring.

Then Paul went on a business trip to Rockford, Illinois. While there, he found an RV dealership and looked at trailers. He called me that evening, bragging about this special one: a 25-foot Holiday Rambler on the showroom floor. Apparently, it was just waiting for us. Paul and I spent two hours on the phone as he described the floor plan and every detail of the trailer. Not only did it have to be functional, it had to be beautiful, too, I insisted. Paul negotiated a discount because it was the end of the season and the next day we owned our first trailer. All this happened in less than a month. When the time is right, everything just clicks.

When we went to pick it up, the dealer spent a lot of time orienting us to all of its features. By the time we finished, I was tired and hungry so I said to Paul, "Let's go to a motel tonight; it is so late." Paul said, "No way" and we checked in to a near-by campground. By the time we got set *up and ate dinner, it was after ten o'clock. It's a day we will never forget!*

We enjoyed this trailer and took many vacations in it. We made improvements: like installing an electric jack to make hooking up to the car easier. Eventually, we had a Hensley Arrow hitch installed to make pulling the trailer even easier. We also put in a water filter.

We even had a consultant come and Feng Shui the trailer. Feng Shui is an ancient Chinese custom to assure you of health, wealth, success, and balance. People around the world have been applying this process to their homes and businesses for centuries, so I decided to cover all bases. The Feng Shui must have worked; we certainly enjoyed many years of fun in this trailer.

Start Small

My advice is to start with a small RV, trailer, or fifth wheel and move up gradually. Make sure you like full-time RVing before you invest a lot of money in a unit. Decide how often you will use it.

Often a couple starts out with the best intentions, then one party or both has a change of heart. Sometimes they have to sell their RV or trailer due to sickness or death. That is why so many used RVs are on the market.

Be cautious, try it out, and do lots of research before buying your RV. You want to be sure RVing suits your lifestyle.

Step 7: Research types, models, and prices of RVs. Here are some options and prices. (See back of book for more information.)

1. **Trailers** (must be pulled by car or truck)
   New – About $19,000 at dealerships
   Used – Check ads in *Trailer Life* and
   Family Motor Coach magazines

2. **Fifth Wheels** (must be pulled by a truck)
   New – Start at $30,000; prices vary depending
   on size
   Used – Check ads in *Trailer Life* and
   Family Motor Coach

3. **Motor Homes**
   New – Start at $60,000 – gas engines
   New – $180,000 to $200,000 and up –
   diesel engines
   Used – Check ads in *Trailer Life* and
   Family Motor Coach. Often, people pull a
   car behind the motor home; of course, this
   requires an additional cost.

We found our 25-foot trailer to be comfortable for weekend trips and month-long vacations and started out on our full-time adventure in our Holiday Rambler.

We had everything we needed packed into every available space. It only had one closet, so a lot of our clothes had to be folded to fit the small storage compartments over the bed. Because of the limited space, we had to choose our wardrobe wisely. The trailer also had some storage under the bed and under the couch. We put extra blankets and outside chairs under the bed. Under the couch we stored our papers and important documents.

We chose our pots and pans carefully: one frying pan, one medium-sized pot, and a few multi-purpose dishes. The trailer was loaded.

We subscribed to a mail service and got our mail every two weeks. The first time, it proved to be a real challenge to find room enough to sort it out. We managed to handle the inconvenience for several weeks. But subconsciously, we must have been thinking we needed a larger unit. Consciously, we felt like we were living in a little dollhouse. In the beginning, we had been so proud of ourselves for having lightened up on material possessions. Maybe we had been unrealistic because we had never lived in such a small space before. So we admitted to each other that someday we'd consider getting a bigger trailer or even a motor coach.

However, it was no coincidence that we went to an RV dealership in North Carolina because we needed a light bulb for our bathroom. We saw several large coaches on the showroom floor of the dealership and fell in love with one. It was very roomy, very beautiful, and well built. We knew that because it was manufactured by the same company as our Holiday Rambler. What's more, it had been reduced in price. We were both surprised that we made the decision to buy it so quickly.

Step 8: Commit to the RV lifestyle before upgrading.

Before you upgrade to a larger trailer or coach, be sure your commitment to this lifestyle is sincere. At the very moment we decided to purchase this new 42-foot motor coach, we made that commitment.

Chapter 4
Take Your Toys

Our first stop was Rend Lake in Illinois. We didn't have reservations but as luck would have it, we were able to find a beautiful, peaceful campsite. The campsite had lots of large shady trees and grass. We parked by beautiful Rend Lake. We brought all our toys. One is our blow-up boat, the Sea Eagle, which inflates to 12 feet by 3 feet. We bought a 3.3 hp motor that fits it perfectly.

The Sea Eagle itself fits into a bag, is easily stored in a car, and can be blown up with a foot pump. The boat comfortably seats two adults only, or two adults and one or two small children. We often take a picnic lunch and tool around for several hours.

We have our golf clubs, diving equipment, tennis racquets, and downhill skis. I am also running my art business out of our trailer, our only home. Our two cell phones and lap top computer allow us to stay in touch with people we need to reach for business and for fun.

On occasion, we have to spend time paying bills. Yes. There are still some bills, especially if you are running a business out of your RV as I am. Thank God for the cell phone. Although it can be frustrating at times, it is a great invention. Cell phones are fine for short calls. But since the cell phone battery can lose its power at any time, long conversations can be trying. Campgrounds usually have a pay phone so having a phone card is better for longer conversations. We find having two cell phones is a necessity so Paul and I can be in touch with each other if one of us goes hiking.

We also have an exercise ball, free weights, and bands with which to do other exercises. In fact, we had a professional trainer set up an exercise program for us so we could stay in shape as we travel.

Having a loose schedule is also the freedom one needs for life on the road. We hold our vision in mind as well as developing our relationship as we travel. We feel so grateful and are determined never to rush again. We want to stop and smell the roses, trees, and grass—to enjoy every minute.

Step 9: Pack Your Toys. These might include:
- Golf clubs
- Ski equipment
- Tennis racquets
- Diving equipment
- Blow-up boat
  (see info at back of book about Sea Eagle)
- Outboard motor

- Exercise equipment: free weights, exercise ball
- Cell phones
- Lap top computer

Find a way to take your interests with you!

Step 10: Set up a mailing system.

The first question everyone asks is, "How do you get your mail?" I discovered a mail forwarding service in Texas. There are others. Wherever you are or expect to be in a few days, you call: 1-800-231-9896 (see Mail Services in the back of this book). There is a nominal fee to join (about $60.00 a year). The service will forward your mail wherever you are and send it any way you wish: regular mail, priority mail, UPS, or Fed-Ex. Of course, you must pay for postage. You can open an account and charge the cost of shipping. If you are expecting a package or mail from a certain party, you may call the service and the representative will tell you if it has arrived in your mailbox.

Tip: We usually get our mail delivered by Fed-Ex 2nd Day Delivery. We belong to an organization called Escapees (see Organizations to Join in the back of this book). They put a $200.00 charge on our credit card to cover our mailing expenses. When the $200.00 is used up, they charge another $200.00. This service is excellent and efficient.

North Carolina/Virginia

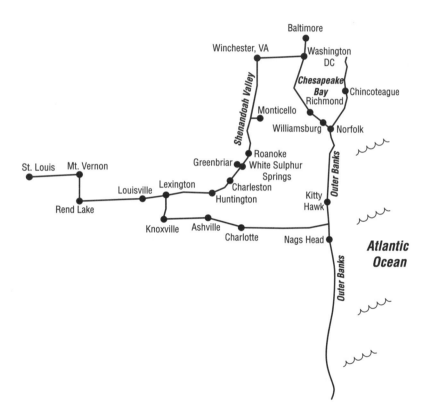

Chapter 5
On the Road Adventuring

*After the three weeks in St. Charles, we went
to Rend Lake for six days and recharged our
batteries through meditation, fresh food, and
exercise of some sort every day. For us, this RV
adventure is about having a simple, healthy life
with little stress. If we feel the need, naps become
part of the everyday routine. I have been praying
for this lifestyle and God has answered our
prayers. Reading, writing this book, and visiting
with my husband is very important to me. I feel
so peaceful and healthy.*

Onward!

New Harmony, Indiana

Taking Highway 14 from Rend Lake, we stopped in New
Harmony, Indiana, which is about 140 miles across Illinois to
Indiana. Established in 1815 as a religious community, it features

traditional communes of people seeking the perfect way of life. New Harmony's residents believe it must be done by separating oneself from the corrupting influences of the larger society.

This conviction is called "utopianism" from Thomas More's book *Utopia*. The book tells of an imaginary kingdom in which people live happily in harmony. The word "utopia" in Greek, means "no place" and suggests that, although no ideal community exists, like-minded people can create one through determination and effort.

George Rapp and his son came from Germany in 1803 and founded the Community of Equality in western Pennsylvania. In 1815, they started a nearby village in Indiana called New Harmony. Then Rapp went back to Pennsylvania and established a village called Economy. After he died in 1847, the village dwindled and was dissolved in 1905.

In New Harmony, we discovered a labyrinth, enclosed in a garden and styled after the labyrinth in Chartes, France. Appropriately, people do meditation and take spiritual walks in a labyrinth.

Since this was the beginning of our soulful and spiritual journey, we walked through the labyrinth saying prayers. It felt really good. It was suggested we walk barefoot; the stone felt rough on my feet—cool in the shade and hot in the sun. The labyrinth symbolizes life. Sometimes life feels good and at other times rough. A person needs to take one step at a time to complete a personal journey. But we are encouraged to keep going toward our destination, even when we are not sure how or why or when we will finish. The whole event was "synchronistic," meaning occurring at the same time.

Santa Claus, Indiana

Santa Claus is about 60 miles from New Harmony. It has a wonderful campground full of wonderful trees. Because we used our "Coast To Coast" discount, it cost us only $6.00 a night, including full hook-ups, water, electric, and sewer.

We spent several perfect days there filled with fun, exercise, prayer, and relaxation. Not surprisingly, we found a wonderful store filled with all kinds of gifts as well as Christmas Trees. There is a post office for mailing postcards marked Santa Claus, Indiana. We had our picture taken in front of a giant Santa, 25-feet tall. We looked like dwarfs in the picture.

Santa Claus also has an amusement park, although we didn't go. But if you are traveling with children or if you like amusement parks and rides, you would enjoy it.

French Lick, Indiana

In this town, we parked our trailer in the hotel's parking lot and stayed at the famous French Lick Hotel for two nights—just for a change of pace. The French Lick Hotel is an elegant hotel about a hundred years old. It has at least two golf courses and great food. It was fun having a big corner room with a big bathtub.

We took a tour of the West Baden Springs Hotel property close by. At one time, it was called the Eighth Wonder of the World. Featuring a dome-shaped building built in 1902, it has seen many events in its history. At one time, this property was owned and operated by Jesuit priests. Later, it became a gambling hotel and, after that, a school. Having been partially restored at a cost of 35 million dollars, it awaits a new buyer who will have to invest several more million to make it habitable, possibly as a hotel again.

Louisville, Kentucky

Just outside of Louisville, in Shelbyville, we found a great open campground called Guist Creek Marine. It has a beautiful lake for boating, plus a lot of space between campsites for playing Frisbee. We launched our blow-up boat the Sea Eagle. Paul's son and family joined us and our grandchildren Sophie and Sammy enjoyed cruising with their Grandpa. When Paul pulled the boat ashore, the children took off their swimsuits and plastered themselves with mud.

We took time to visit our daughter-in-law's family, where we were wined and dined. Joan, our daughter-in-law, is one of six children in that family, so when all the spouses and grandchildren get together, it is quite a fun-filled group. Connie, the Mom of the bunch, is a special friend and very gracious lady.

Lexington, Kentucky

On to Troy Pike, near Lexington. My brother and sister-in-law have a wonderful horse farm there and we enjoyed fun and laughs with them. We love the flexibility, freedom, and convenience we have with our Merrily We Roll Along to go and see people.

We spent four days at "Bit O Blarney" Horse Farm on 90 acres in the beautiful, rolling hills of Kentucky. There, they breed and board many horses. It was a relaxing break to visit with the family and watch the horses. Several horses had had foals. Our niece Maureen was responsible for training and riding several horses. Our nephew Brian and his new wife Veda were there, also. Being with family is one of the focuses of our travels and adventures.

We have family and friends all over the country. As we travel, we take time to visit people we care about. Since we have our own living space with all the conveniences, we do not impose on anyone. We usually find a nearby campground, spend time with people we know, then go back to our trailer. We know that houseguests get old after three days. You have heard the fish story: houseguests and fish stink after three days.

Chapter 6
The Light Bulb Story

Charlotte, NC

We were on to Charlotte, North Carolina, to visit some wonderful friends Karen and Jim Schomaker. On the way, we stayed in an Escapee Trailer Park in the Knoxville, Tennessee, area and a Coast To Coast trailer park called Pride Resort in the Waynesville, NC area. Both were highly recommended.

Close to Charlotte, we realized we needed a light bulb for the bathroom and saw a large RV dealership just outside Hendersonville. When we got there, Paul headed for the parts department. I, on the other hand, headed for all the beautiful new motor homes on display in the large showroom. One especially caught my eye—without a doubt the most beautiful, luxurious motor home I had ever seen. Coincidentally, they had a reduced price on it.

Paul and I both fell in love with it. No shopping, no looking around. We bought it on the spot. The coach was to be ready for delivery in two weeks. Perfect timing—this would give us just enough time to visit friends in Charlotte as well as visit with our daughter Kathleen in Florida.

Our new coach—a Navigator also built by Holiday Rambler—is 42 feet long and has every imaginable convenience device on it. Having the

extra space and extra storage is great. We feel fortunate to be able to afford such a magnificent piece of machinery.

We spent two days with our friend Dianna Nix as well as with Karen and Jim Schomaker. Good friends are another reason for "full timing"—it gives us a chance to re-connect with many people and realize how lucky we are to have such great relationships. And our cell phone and our lap top computer allow us to always be in touch with our family and friends.

It was no accident we were looking for a "light bulb" for our trailer and found the "perfect" Holiday Rambler Motor Home.

I recall one of the days we spent in North Carolina starting off great. We went for a walk, ate lunch, and ran some errands including going to the post office. Unfortunately, we had left the car unlocked. When we came back to the trailer, I looked around for my wallet, my checkbook, and my cell phone because I thought I had left them there. But I couldn't find any of them. I then realized they had been stolen. What a mess!

We believed it happened when we'd gone to the Post Office, so we reported the theft to the post office staff as well as the South Carolina and North Carolina police (since our campground was in North Carolina and the Post Office was in South Carolina). Then I started calling the credit card companies. Indeed, the robbers were having a hey-day charging thousands of dollars in only six hours. The Lesson: Lock The Car and Don't Be Too Trusting!

It is a shame people have to steal to get the "stuff" they feel they need at another's expense. At least it made me realize that WE have it all: each other and our health, specifically. That's what is important. And maybe this incident tested our priorities, as life always does.

Paul and I had a lot to learn about operating our new motor home. We had to test-drive it to get comfortable with its handling on the road. Driving a large motor home as well as pulling a Chevy Tahoe took a lot of getting use to. All hooked up, we cover about 65 feet of road space.

Merrily Two is positively gorgeous—black, gold, beige, and white on the outside with imaginative graphics. On the inside, the couch and carpets are off-white; the chairs are an off-white leather. The floor (other than the carpeted area in the living room and the bedroom) is ceramic tile while the counter tops are Corian. In the bathroom, I have my own vanity and sink, and Paul has his own. The shower has a skylight above it. A large mirrored closet holds our hanging clothes and we have plenty of drawers and cabinets for folding clothes. The décor is light and bright. Walnut wood accents are found throughout the coach.

The motor coach has three zones for heating and cooling, a spacious double-door refrigerator and double-door freezer, and a combination microwave/convection oven that makes food preparations quick and easy. We also have a small oven under the three-burner cook top. It's oh so nice to have a roomy kitchen. And I love the washer and dryer. It sure beats the campground laundries.

The surround sound stereo system, CD players, and VCR make our new home even more comfortable. We have a back up rear vision camera, which we use to help back into parking places. We also have a large automatic awning, which retracts on its own when the wind gets higher than 18 miles an hour.

While sitting outside under the awning, we can pull out the TV (one of three), which is in one of the pull-out bays under the coach. and watch TV or movies on the VCR.

Chapter 7
Southeastern Adventures

Sarasota, Florida

Before we picked up Merrily Two, we flew into Sarasota to visit our daughter Kathleen and her friend Mitch, then joined them on their new sailboat.

We were on their boat and sailing smoothly when all of a sudden, the chain came off the tiller wheel and we had to use the tiller bar. We experienced a few anxious moments, but Mitch, the captain, did a great job of averting a crisis. With crewmembers Kathleen and Paul, Mitch got control of the boat and we sailed safely into port.

Sarasota, a beautiful town on the water, has beaches that are wide and inviting, with lots of delicious restaurants to suit every taste and great shopping at St. Armand's Circle. If you like boating of any variety, you will love Sarasota. The weather is ideal in the winter months, though very hot in June.

Once we got going in our new coach, we made North Carolina's Jelly Stone Park our next stop. It had been raining for several days. We pulled into our campsite just a few feet off of the exact "pad." After eating a quick lunch, we were about to get hooked up when Paul looked at the

*left side of the coach and noticed it had SUNK
18 to 20 inches into the mud. Not a pretty sight.
Weighing about 50 thousand pounds, we
knew we had a challenge on our hands. How do
we get this coach upright? We called AAA.
Unfortunately, we didn't have RV towing insurance with AAA, however, it was included with
our motor coach insurance. Through the company RV Allliance and our AAA information,
we found a wrecker. Four hours later, with the
wrecker and Paul's knowledge and lots of
prayers, Merrily Two found level ground. We
decided to move our campsite to one with more
gravel. Of course, this episode was the talk of the
whole campground. What a way to meet people.*

Oldest Lighthouse at Cape Hatteras

The Outer Banks is a "must see" and so is the Cape Hatteras
seashore. It is rather crowded as only one or two roads go
North and South. My advice is this: "Don't be in a hurry."
Like most visitors, we went to see the tallest and oldest light-
house at Cape Hatteras. Of course, we climbed to the top.
What a view of the Atlantic!

This is a very famous lighthouse that was recently moved from its original site because of erosion.

Kitty Hawk, N.C

At Kitty Hawk, naturally, we visited the Wright Brothers Museum and concluded that Orville and Wilber Wright were definitely ahead of their time. (The museum fee is $2.00 to $4.00 depending if you are over 62 years old and show a Golden Age Pass. See information in the back.)

In 1903, Orville Wright telegraphed home the triumphant news of the first powered flight. The news was dispatched from Kitty Hawk. But actually the flight took place four miles south from the base of Kill Devil Hill.

Inside the museum was a replica of the original plane. Outside there were markers showing the distance of each of the three flights the Wright Brothers had actually flown their plane. The museum had the history of how they had come to invent the plane. They had had a bicycle shop and were interested in photography. On the property was a monument built to honor their achievement. We felt fortunate and very moved to experience such an historical event.

Ever since Wilber and Orville put Kitty Hawk on the map as "the birthplace of aviation," it has become one the largest townships on the Outer Banks. On the Oceanside, thousands of rental homes, restaurants, and shops have sprung up to make this area popular for vacationers.

Williamsburg, Virginia

Williamsburg was about three hours from our last stop at Grandy, N.C. We stayed at Chickahominy Riverfront Park in Williamsburg.

The campground is on the Chickahominy River. It was great fun floating in our inflatable boat, the Sea Eagle. We went up the river for about five miles. It was very scenic ride with beautiful houses along the way. As we approached the James River, which at this point is about a mile across, the water became very choppy and we turned around and went back to the campground. The James River is an interesting waterway. It becomes Hampton Roads where it flows into the Chesapeake Bay, which is where ships from WWII are mothballed. The fleet anchored at the Norfolk Naval Yards are also here.

We went to Colonial Williamsburg and walked around, then ate dinner at one of the historic eating-places from the 1800s where Jefferson and Washington ate. Quaint Williamsburg has been beautifully restored with homes, shops, gardens, and streets from the 1800s. A "must see" for history buffs.

People from all over the world come to visit to see, with the help of authentic period guides, where history was made. Visitors experience first-hand the times and lives of European settlers coming to the "New Land." The Historic Area of Williamsburg is centered around the Duke of Gloucester Street.

Guides dressed in period costumes summon you inside the eating-places in Williamsburg, which are so authentic that you expect Washington or Jefferson to waltz in any minute. The servers, also dressed in 1800s garb, speak as they did during that time. The menus include dishes served in those times. As you walk up and down the streets, you see people dressed in long dresses, tall hats, and clothing of the period. Even the shopkeepers were dressed in period clothing.

In certain historic areas, visitors can attend actual performances about various facets of colonial life throughout the week. The College of William and Mary—the college that Thomas Jefferson attended—can be found just down the Duke of Gloucester Street. This College began the Honor Society as well as the Phi Beta Kappa Society.

We certainly felt that we had stepped back in time and became part of a movie that was 200 years old.

Tip: When you are a member of Coast to Coast or any camping organization, that park at which you join becomes your "home park." At your "home park," you get two weeks free camping every year with a Coast to Coast membership. Depending on where you are traveling, you don't ever have to stay at your "home park." After paying the initial membership dues, you only pay $6.00 a night at all Coast to Coast campgrounds. That includes full hook-ups with water, electric, and sewer. The price is a great deal if you can find Coast to Coast campgrounds as you travel. Members receive a full directory of sites around the country.

The Chickahominy Riverfront Park, just outside of Williamsburg, is on a peaceful river ideal for fishing or just boating up and down. We spent a perfect day there, very quiet and very peaceful. We are getting into this life-style nicely.

Time takes on a new meaning when one is always on vacation. I have to look at the calendar to see what day it is. When we get up in the morning, we exercise first, then decide if we need to take care of chores or get in touch with people. Since I am running my business out of the coach, I need to spend time on the phone or do some bookwork. We then check out the area for points of interest. Often we just decide to read a book or do nothing. Days just fly by . . . and it's all fun.

Chapter 8
Presidential Lifestyle

Washington, D.C.

Next, we headed for our nation's capital city. In Washington, we stayed at Cherry Hills RV Park, which I would highly recommend. Its amenities include modem hook-ups, two swimming pools, and a café. It is in a great location near highways and near the Metro underground subway in the downtown D.C. area. Because of this great location, we were able to connect with cousins and friends we had not seen in 15 years or more. We saw the Vietnam and Korean War Memorials—impressive—and the White House—beautiful. Of course, everyone wants to see these, which are wonderful, but the Holocaust Museum is a MUST. I will always have haunting memories of this sobering, sad reminder of world history.

We found people in D.C. to be helpful. Here's an example. As we studied our map on a downtown corner, a man stopped and offered to help us find the way to one of the Smithsonian Museums—the Air and Space Museum. We found this museum, the National History Museum, and the National Shrine are all-worthwhile places to visit.

We found the Metro to be an easy, wonderful way to get around and we recommend avoiding driving in downtown D.C.

All in all, Washington D.C. is a great city full of education, beauty, and culture. It also has great food! We ate steamed crabs twice. Thank goodness Paul had taught me how to eat them; it requires a definite technique. But the result is well worth all the effort—so delicious!

Shenendoah Valley

We left the Washington, D.C. area and headed for Front Royal in the Shenendoah Valley, where the mountains are exceptionally beautiful. We enjoyed staying at the Skyline Ranch Resort in Front Royal, Virginia. It is a peaceful Coast to Coast campground (cost: $6.00 a night). From here, it's easy to go hiking in Shenendoah National Park, which is a treat. Virginia is a beautiful state; don't miss it. Skyline Cave near the campground is another must see in the Shenendoah Valley area.

Charlottesville, Virginia

Monticello, President Thomas Jefferson's home, is an educational experience not to be missed. It features Civil War battlefields nearby and memorabilia from that era. People can enjoy reenactments of the time. The mountains and valleys are a beautiful sight for everyone to enjoy. The third President of the U.S., Jefferson was futuristic, as shown by the architectural design of his home, Monticello. It is masterpiece that was designed and redesigned, built and rebuilt over a total of 40 years. It has a domed roof, which was influenced by the new architecture seen in France. Unfortunately, Jefferson died in debt. His daughter had to sell the furnishings and then the plantation itself. The estate of 522 acres and home sold for $4,500 in 1831. It is now owned by the Thomas Jefferson Foundation.

We found the whole area of Virginia and West Virginia to be a desirable destination because of its mountains, streams, moderate climate, and history.

The Greenbrier, White Sulphur Springs, West Virginia

The Greenbrier or "The Briar," as my brother-in law calls it, is quite "The Place." An elegant hotel that offers anything one might desire, this 200-year-old resort is still owned by the C & O/B & O Railroad. In fact, from the main entrance, it looks like the White House in Washington. And its grounds are manicured to the last blade of grass.

Tennis, golf lessons, and gourmet cooking classes are only a few of the dozens of activities available. Pampering at all levels is at your beck and call. Of course, the shopping and restaurants are more than outstanding. We ate a delicious casual lunch at the Sam Snead's Tavern & Restaurant, named after the resort's golf pro of many years. The restaurant overlooks the golf course. What a view! We also stayed for "High Tea" and enjoyed the music, tea, and crumpets in elegant style. Then we headed back to our coach to have our modest roll-ups for dinner.

We love every minute of this new lifestyle and are so grateful for the opportunity to see this great land of ours. At first when we sold our home and everything in it, I felt skeptical. Were we doing something drastic that we might regret? But as we get into this new way of life, we get excited about what is to come next. There is so much to see and

so many people we want to visit. I hope we have enough time to see and do everything.

We find the freedom of taking our home with us everywhere we go is exhilarating. We have no grass to cut, no state taxes to pay (or at least no state taxes in Texas, where we have our permanent address). Leaving my home and everything I loved definitely stretched my courage. But no matter how hard it was, I want to declare that it can be done and it's worth every ounce of energy it takes. Our new lifestyle has given us a new lease on life. Because we have met so many interesting, exciting people, we have become more interesting and exciting ourselves. What's more, we feel so young and vibrant.

My advice to you, if this lifestyle interests you, is just to do it. There will always be people around to help you.

Chapter 9
Going Home to St. Louis

Going home is so much fun. I need to touch base every few months because of our family, friends, and connections of a lifetime. Specifically, we came back to St. Louis to help my mother celebrate her 87th birthday. She didn't expect to see us so we really surprised her. Everyone at the church reception welcomed us with open arms, which really felt good.

On this trip home, I attended to business and worked with my assistant Lindsey Andrews. Then we hosted a fabulous party at the RV Park; we invited 100 people and enjoyed visiting with all of our loved ones.

Dorothy was so right in the Wizard of Oz
when she said, "There is no place like home."

Niagara Region

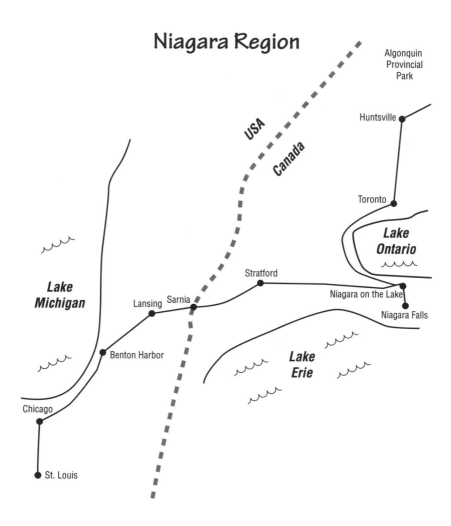

Chapter 10
North to Cool Canada

Stratford, Ontario, Canada

We left St. Louis when it was about 106 degrees F. so we wanted to zoom due north into Canada and cool off. First, we stopped in Paw Paw, Michigan, to see some old friends. Then we headed north, arriving in Stratford, Ontario, the next day.

Stratford is a wonderful town filled with beautiful flowers and parks and the Avon River running through it. This "slice of England" right over the border is even complete with works of Shakespeare and other playwrights at the Stratford Festival.

We enjoyed perfect weather in August—a temperature of 72 degrees F. and no humidity. We parked outside the city at the Wildwood Provincial Park. With its hiking trails and a swimming pool, beautiful trees and lawns, and its spaciousness between campsites, Wildwood is especially wonderful for camping in a tent or a trailer. We hiked, rested, and relaxed there. What a life.

We spent three days going to the Festival Theater in Stratford. We saw "The Three Musketeers," which was great fun, and Gilbert and Sullivan's "Patience," a wonderful musical opera. We also went to "The Diary of Anne Frank," a haunting story about Jews hiding out during the Hitler years and the indomitable human spirit. I will remember it forever. I, too, want to be remembered for helping people. Anne Frank gave others courage, just like I hope this book gives people courage to easily and gently run away from home.

Meeting nice people is another bonus of camping. People are friendly and helpful. We see that we are all in this together. So it doesn't matter if you have a small tent, pop-up camper, or big RV. Campers are all in this adventure together!

Algonquin Park in Dwight, Ontario

About 200 miles north from Stratford on Highway 60 (east of Highway 11 and north of Toronto) is Algonquin Trails Campground (also a Coast to Coast campground for $6.00 a night). Right next to Algonquin Park, this campground has large wooded sites, water, and electric hook-ups with boating, canoeing, and hiking nearby. It gets our "two thumbs up" rating and so does the peaceful environment in the park. The air is crisp and clean, temperature cool, no humidity—really heaven on earth.

Hikes throughout Algonquin Park feature some incredible waterfalls. One of the hikes goes to Mizzy Lake. What started out to be an hour-long hike ended up being 2 1/2 hours filled with challenges. Undaunted, we kept on going and reached an art gallery in the park displaying several wildlife artists' work. By then, our feet were numb but nearby we found the Barclay Inn. From the Inn, a boat takes diners across the lake to a restaurant. Luckily, we arrived in perfect time to catch the boat for the first of only two seatings. Another couple waited at the boat dock, too, so we started chatting with them and ate dinner together. Ken and Mary were celebrating their 37th anniversary. As I have said many times, there are no accidents and many pleasant surprises.

Nice people, fun experiences. Expect the best and you get it.

Paul's Birthday, September 9th

We celebrated Paul's B-Day quietly. Paul received birthday wishes from all the kids. I know I should be waiting on him, but he is the cook on the Merrily Two. I have got it made and I know it! The pancakes he made were awesome, as usual.

We launched The Sea Eagle because the day was perfect for boating on Algonquin's spectacular lakes. We boated around one of the lakes where we could view many beautiful homes with boat docks. Once we got back to our coach, we visited with neighbors, fixed pizza and salad, and fell deeply tired into bed. "It was a perfect B-Day," Paul said.

We spent the next few days resting, hiking, exercising, and meditating. We listened to a tape of Rev. Phyllis Clay Sparks, our minister from "The Soul Esteem" church in St. Louis. We get the tapes from the services. Since we can't always go to church, getting tapes of the services is the next best thing.

When you are on the road, exercising, walking, and meditation should become a part of your daily routine. Staying healthy and in shape takes a lot of discipline, but I can't emphasize enough how important this is to your being happy while traveling.

Ottawa, Ontario

On to Ottawa and the Hither Hills Campground, just outside of the city. A pretty city, Ottawa is the capital of Canada. It shows off flowers everywhere, especially around the Parliament Buildings, which look very impressive. On Parliament Hill stand the Royal Canadian Mint and the Supreme Court of Canada. Some museums in Ottawa are the National Museum of Science and Technology, The National Aviation Museum (housing more than 100 aircraft), and the Canadian Museum of Nature.

As we walked around the downtown area, we found the Sparks Street Mall, which is closed to vehicles. There we found exclusive boutiques and specialty shops, restaurants, and outdoor cafes. The whole city reminds me of Paris. We found a wonderful outdoor Farmer's Market, Bayward Market, where we bought lots of fruits and vegetables. Farmers have been bringing their produce to this location since 1830. A bike path follows the canal throughout the city. In the winter, the canal becomes a long ice-skating rink.

All in all, Ottawa is another "must see" place.

Quebec City, Quebec

It was raining the day we arrived in Quebec City, but that didn't stop us. It is also like Paris with its narrow, cobblestone streets and quaint restaurants. Flowers are everywhere. We both had our hair cut at the famous Fairmont Château Frontenac Hotel, a charming hotel about 200 years old. We ate dinner at a quaint restaurant in the historic district downtown. The restaurant was built to resemble a wine cave.

As we walked around historic Quebec City, we saw the copper rooftops and the cobblestone streets of the early years. The 17th and 18th century buildings have been restored and converted for residential and commercial use today. You can get a good view by taking a scenic cruise down the St. Lawrence River.

Basilique Cathedrale Notre Dame de Quebec is the fruit of 350 years of work. The richly decorated basilica features stained glass windows, an Episcopal throne dais, and many beautiful paintings.

St. Anne de Beupre, 30 miles east of Quebec City, is one of Canada's most famous Catholic Shrines and places of pilgrimage. St. Anne was the mother of Mary and the grandmother of Jesus. The chapel was built in 1658 on a piece of land donated by Messr Elienne de Lessard. Over the years, millions of pilgrims have come to this place. It's located parallel to the St. Lawrence and is visible for miles from both sides of the river.

The Statue of St. Anne is also known as the Statue of Miracles. The stones of the church gently whisper of the joys, hopes, fears, and pain of all those who have placed their prayers before the Lord. People come to the shine to find the deeper meaning of life through meditation and prayerful solitude.

The basement houses a large replica of Michelangelo's Pieta; the original is in St. Peter's Basilica in Rome.

We spent a lot of enjoyable time walking around the grounds, which contain bronze sculptures of The Way Of The Cross.

It kept raining in Quebec for several days. Finally, the sun came out and we went for a bike ride along a beautiful bike path that ran parallel to a creek. We ended the day by eating Chef Paul's clam chowder and Anita's famous salad.

During our time in Quebec, we stayed at Un Air d'ete Campground, about 20 minutes outside of the city. It's another Coast to Coast campground that charges only $6.00 a night. The area, surrounded by farms and forests, is only four miles to Pont Rouge.

Quebec has a European flavor in its architecture and restaurants as well as its history, which makes visiting this area a memorable experience.

Pont Rouge, Quebec

Near our campground is the town of Pont Rouge, where the people are friendly and helpful, the homes are well cared for, and flowers are everywhere. Pont Rouge has a great IGA market with the best pizzas I have ever eaten. Pont Rouge means "red bridge." There is, indeed, a bridge that the town was named after. We had no trouble communicating with any of the people in this quaint town because they speak English as well as French. I can see why people are so happy in this small town that we grew to love. It has a comfortable atmosphere, and many services are within walking distance from the residential area.

We traveled in Canada for about a month in late August and early September. We faced no crowds wherever we went and the temperatures and people were great.

New England Area

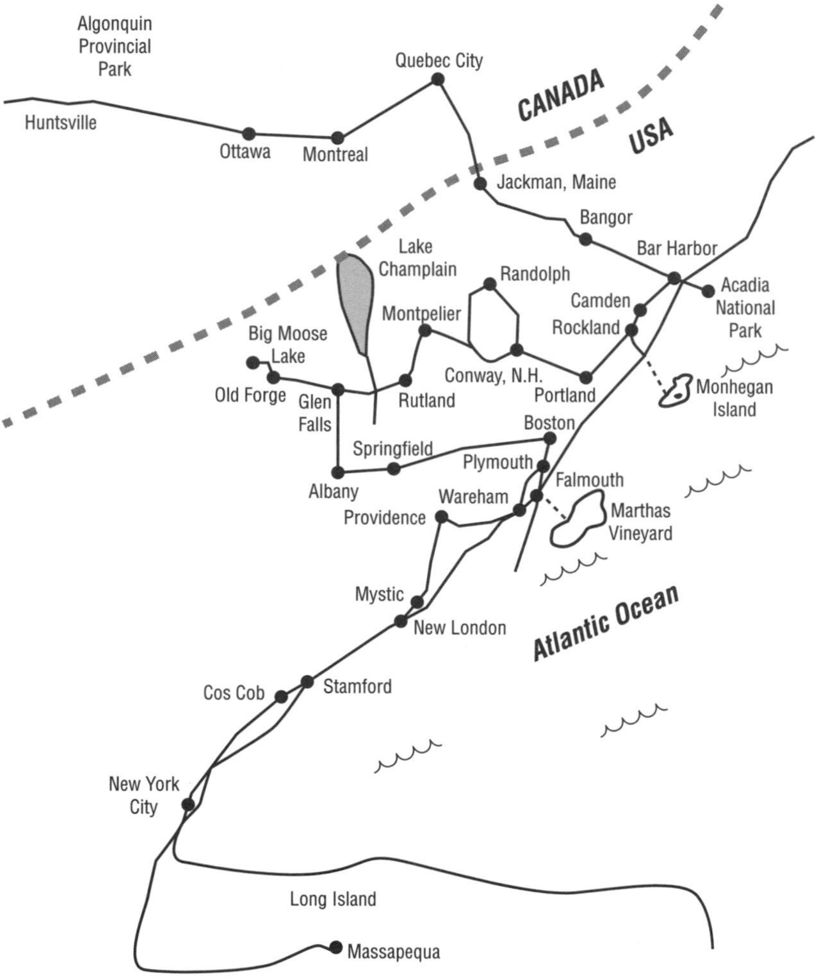

Chapter 11
New England Area

Jackman, Maine

The first city we came to across the Canadian border was Jackman, Maine. We found a beautiful and peaceful place, the Moose Valley Campground, just two miles outside of town. Again, the people there were so friendly and helpful.

It was September, the first day of fall, and cool in northern Maine. We ate a delicious meal at a famous four-star restaurant named Moose Point. The restaurant overlooked the lake and we could view mountains in the background. I felt like we were back in Homer, Alaska, on the Cook Inlet. (Homer is my favorite place in the world . . . so far.) People from all over the globe come to Moose Point. I can certainly understand why.

We took a ride down Highway 201 for about 26 miles until we came to many beautiful lakes and rivers where people rent houses and go boating. In the summer, this area would be very busy but not in the fall when the leaves start to turn— the perfect time for a visit. We walked in the crisp, clean air along a path that follows the lake—a healthy place for your body, spirit, and mind. It felt so invigorating. *Thank you God, for such a wonderful opportunity to be in this place.*

Rangeley, Maine

Nearly Rangeley, we stayed at a secluded and peaceful campground near Lake Aziscohos called Black Brook Cove. It was so remote, we had no phone service.

Rangeley and Farmington have many big old homes, several of which have been turned into businesses. Visitors can easily find restaurants, coffee shops, and the usual other stores. These towns are so small and charming, we felt like the clocks had been turned back 100 years.

We took a ride to Eustes, Maine, then continued to Kingsly where we found the Stanley Steamer Museum. The Stanley brothers, who were twins, not only invented the steam-powered engine automobile at the turn of the century, but also developed a process for developing photographs. This process was sold to Eastman who started Eastman Kodak. Again, we learn so much from traveling.

I needed to take a "time out" after straining my back cleaning house and searched for a chiropractor. After asking around, I located Dr. Roberts in Farmington, where the University of Maine is. Luckily, I felt better in just a few days, thanks to him.

Bar Harbor, Maine, and Acadia National Park

Acadia National Park is one of the most breathtaking places I have ever seen. It features Cadillac Mountain, which is 1532 feet high—the highest point on the Atlantic Coast of North America. This place is not to be missed.

Bar Harbor is a busy commercial tourist town full of shops and restaurants offering great lobster, seafood, and clam chowder, of course. There are many campgrounds from which to choose as well as biking and hiking trails. Though rainy and cool when we rolled in, it was still beautiful.

North East Harbor is in the Bar Harbor area. My favorite place was the Smart Gallery, run by a talented, well-known water colorist named Winnie Smart. She has two galleries, one in Bar Harbor, Maine, and the other in Boca Grande, Florida.

Paul rode his bike; I chose to hike. What I thought was going to be an hour-long hike turned out to be three hours of agony. Several times while hiking around Eagle Lake (without a map), I thought I was lost. Everyone I asked for directions was so helpful and I tried not to panic, yet I was getting tired. At one point, I was about to sit down and cry. Then I saw a man on a bike and he assured me I was going the right way. I kept stopping bicycle riders and asking them how much farther to the main road. The road was actually a network of carriage paths so that made giving any directions confusing. Finally, finally, Paul came to look for

*me. I was so relieved to see him after thinking
that I may never lay eyes on him again. It was
scary, but at least the story had a happy ending.
I have learned an important lesson: Carry a
map when hiking in a strange place.*

Camden and Rockland, Maine

Camden is a quaint coastal town full of B & Bs, antique shops, galleries, coffee houses, restaurants, and beautiful boats. Camden is named The Jewel of the Sea.

Rockland is another seaport town just a few miles from Camden. There, one can catch a Windjammer cruise for three to four days or get on a boat for a few hours to see the coast of Maine. Do not miss the opportunity to take a boat to Monhegan Island. No cars are allowed on this island and only about 75 people live there year round. It has many hiking trails as well as hotels and B& Bs because people love to stay for several days.

Wonderful art museums are sprinkled throughout this cultured area, including Andrew Wyeth's exhibit in Rockland.

The Farnsworth Art Museum is one of the finest regional art museums in the country with a specialized collection focusing on Maine's role in American art. The museum's collections mirror the history of Maine, its people, their occupations and values. It includes art by Winslow Homer, Maurice Prendergast, Andrew Wyeth, and Jamie Wyeth.

The museum plays a vital role in the cultural life of the state and serves as a valuable resource for studying Maine and American art. School children across the state and in outlying island communities come to the museum regularly.

New Hampshire

The White Mountains of New Hampshire are awesome. We decided to stay in the Twin Mountain area for five days. I'm told only two places in the world have such brilliant colors when the fall leaves start to turn: New England and Japan. And here we were, in the midst of the best.

Besides driving and hiking, we love the theater and go whenever we have the opportunity. So in North Conway, we saw Neil Simon's "Chapter Two." Community theater is often excellent because it supports the culture of the small town. Talented local people are given a chance to use their skills. Often, young actors and actresses are brought in from other communities as well as from Europe before they go on to Broadway. I believe travelers should support the theater and the arts in small towns to keep the culture alive.

It is important to keep the adventure exciting and fun, which is why Littleton, New Hampshire (near Twin Mountain) was worth checking out. An historic town, it has been noted as being one of the most interesting small towns. In the heart of the White Mountains, Littleton prides itself as the best place to work, raise a family, and own a business. It is centrally located to Boston, Mass., Montreal, Burlington, Vt. and Portland, Maine.

Littleton has a 100-year-old opera house and a fall calendar of cultural activities for the whole family. The town also has a low crime rate and claims to have the lowest utility rates in the North East. We found a great health food store, The Healthy Rhino. We also enjoyed going into the Mt. Washington Hotel, built in 1902.

At one point, we made a wrong turn because I looked at the map incorrectly. We ended up in a construction zone and that delayed our arrival at our campground by about an hour.

I find that if and when this happens and anyone gets frustrated (especially me), it's important to make no big deal of it. Then everyone can stay happier and more relaxed.

Rutland, Vermont

Vermont has lots of rivers and lakes, and is known for its Green Mountains. We found a small but nice campground in Rutland, Vermont and got the last "full hook-up" site—perfect timing once again. From people we met there, we learned that Abraham Lincoln's son, Robert Todd Lincoln, his only child that lived into adulthood, had a summer mansion called Hildene, built in Manchester, Vermont, about 1902. Manchester is full of beautiful old homes, shops, restaurants, B & Bs, and hotels—a charming town not to be skipped.

A day I have long awaited came while we were in Vermont.

Being an art dealer, I represent Charlie Cramer, an outstanding photographer from Santa Clara, California. We had been doing business for nine years and knew each other well . . . on the phone. He and a friend had been in this area photographing the fall foliage. Today, we got to meet in person. And it felt like we had known each other forever. A bonus!

The Adirondacks, New York

We stayed at Seventh Lake, a State Park in the Adirondacks, and wanted to visit our friends Doris and Tom Hartz, who live on Big Moose Lake. Their house is accessible only by boat. Their property is closest to Inlet, New York. We spent an enjoyable evening with them. The next day, we hiked around their property, which is preserved by the State of New York. No one is allowed to develop any part of the land.

While there, we went out to dinner at The Big Moose Restaurant (a famous cookbook came from there). We also went to a Mountain Man Rendezvous where frontiersmen dressed in traditional clothes from the 1700s and 1800s. They slept in wigwams and prepared food over the fires as they did back then. We saw knife-throwing competitions, which were popular in the olden days. Many of their crafts were for sale as were animal skins and implements. The rendezvous lasted for a week, with people camping out there the whole time.

Plymouth, Massachusetts

This is where the famous Plymouth Rock is found, where the pilgrims who came over from England on a ship called the Mayflower landed. Today, Plymouth is a quaint town on the Atlantic Ocean, centrally located not far from Boston and Martha's Vineyard, Nantucket, and Cape Cod. We stayed at the Pinewood Campground just outside of Plymouth. There, the campsites are so large, we felt like we were staying right in the woods.

Martha's Vineyard

We took the ferry over to Martha's Vineyard for the day, a delightful sunshiny day. The best way to get a good overview of the island is to take the Island Tour. There are many lavish private estates including the famous Kennedy estate and those of other notable people.

Myles Standish State Park

This majestic park near Plymouth offers many hiking paths so that's what we set out to do. We stopped first at a ranger station to get some maps and ask for suggestions. One of the rangers said, "It is really not a good idea to hike because the hunters might mistake you for deer." Needless to say, we cancelled our idea about hiking for the day.

Tip: Be sure to check out the hunting season dates before you hike in a new place.

Boston, Massachusetts

We took the commuter train to Boston and got off at Park Street where the Freedom Trail begins. (The commuter train is a great idea when going into Boston; you do not want to drive on the busy Boston streets if you can avoid it.) We walked the Red Line around the historic area and saw the famous North Church and the USS Constitution. The Freedom Trail (or the Red Line) takes tourists through various parts of the downtown area on a guided walking tour. The JFK Library is very impressive, very moving, and very educational—a "must see" if you are anywhere near Boston.

Renaissance Festival near Plymouth, Massachusetts

If the opportunity to attend a Renaissance Festival ever presents itself, take it. What an event. It happens for six weeks every fall in this area. Many adults and children wear costumes from Medieval Renaissance days. The Festival highlights entertainment, food (of course), and period events. For example, we enjoyed an authentic jousting match. From swords to tattoos, something for everyone was available for sale. Festival grounds were set up amazingly well to accommodate thousands of visitors.

Fair Haven and New Bedford, Massachusetts

Our friends, the Giblins, took us on an extensive walking and driving tour of this area, which they knew well because they had grown up here. The famous Whaling Museum has been recently renovated and features the largest Blue Whale skeleton in the world. Textile mills were once located in New Bedford. This charming seacoast town is definitely worth a visit, especially if you have good friends there like we do. We enjoy visiting people like the Giblins whom we haven't seen in many years.

Mystic, Connecticut

The Mystic Seaport is so full of history. It is the United States' leading maritime museum, guardian of the largest collections of boats and nautical photography in the world. Mystic seaport features a unique shipyard where the nearly lost art of wooden shipbuilding endures. It has a 19th century village, tall ships, historic buildings, and exhibit galleries overflowing with the culture of seafaring life. There is a great gift shop and many fine restaurants.

We also visited the Mashantucket Pequot Museum and Research Center, which has an exhibit of a 400-year-old Indian Village, one of the largest single exhibits in the world. Using 51 life-like figures, the Village features the latest in 3D computer interactives.

We had a stressful few minutes at Mystic when I lost my cell phone. It had fallen out of my pocket. Luckily, Paul, the hero, found it in the parking lot.

Chapter 12
Travels in New York State

Bethpage, New York

At Bethpage on Long Island, we stayed at a spacious campground for a week, visiting family and friends and went to my great nephew's Bar Mitzvah. Once again, we had the opportunity to be with family and friends in the city.

Taking the train into New York City from Hicksville, we got off at Penn Station. We ate pastrami sandwiches at a New York deli, walked to Times Square, Central Park and down Fifth Avenue. What a busy, exciting city—lots of fun and lots of people, to put it mildly. We had dinner with a friend, Colleen McGrath, at Roc, a great Italian restaurant in Soho. The food was outstanding.

We met Katie and Dean Everard, friends we had originally met in Italy five years ago. They are both photographers. We continued to enjoy spending time with our cousins Joe and Sandy Bolze. Cathy La Porte, Paul's former secretary, joined us for dinner. She brought us a delicious cake, too. When we haven't seen people in ages, they treat us like celebrities.

The Bar Mitzvah festivities began with
temple services Friday night. It was wonderful to
see all the people who had come from far and

near to celebrate my great nephew Alex
Goldberg's Bar Mitzvah. The festivities contin-
ued throughout the weekend, including the
service Saturday that was led by Alex and the
Rabbi. Alex is an articulate, smart, and person-
able young man who spoke Hebrew well. He
had been taking Hebrew lessons for seven years
and it showed.

In Alex's speech, he mentioned that his
"Jerusalem" was going to "sleep away" camp. On
the other hand, his "Egypt" was school. I felt
that statement was insightful and profound,
especially for a 13-year-old young man. To find
"our Jerusalem" is a mission for all of us. To seek
and find what we love and enjoy is so impor-
tant. I really believe God wants us to find and
know our "Jerusalem," however long it takes.
Don't give up until you find it! I learned so
much from my nephew. We are all each other's
teachers, no matter what age.

Bye, Bye to New York

We left New York early Sunday to get out of town and traffic. Since we had stayed up past midnight on Saturday, we were very tired. After driving all day, we arrived in Pennsylvania. By the time we found a campground, it was after dark. We advise people not to travel after dark. We don't always listen to our own advice!

After parking and plugging into the electric, we found out there was no water on this site. It had been turned off for the season. When we were about to fix dinner, everything shut down. Paul, the mechanic and coach driver, was stumped. He tried everything he knew to get the power to work. The generator didn't get the system going either. We had no water pump. That means no toilet, no water, no shower, and no water to wash dishes. No heat.

Okay, what do we do now? We got out the manual, then called Bruce, the technician at Ledford's where we bought the coach. We had his home number but unfortunately he wasn't home. So we called Bob Morton, the salesman at Ledford's. He wasn't home, either. Now what?

Paul was beside himself. I went into my praying mode. We were prepared to go to bed with all our clothes on and hope the system would correct itself in the morning. I was saying my prayers—Big Time. And I kept calling

Bruce, hoping he would get home soon. It was getting chillier in the coach. Paul decided to try to get it working once again. He started the coach and put it in gear. Like "A Miracle," the lights came on. We had water and heat. Everything was fine again.

I really believe it was the prayers that did it. We were so grateful!!! We took some deep breaths and sighed with relief. We took showers and had a good night's sleep. When we finally reached Bruce by phone, he said we might have a "solonoid" going bad. This would cause all the systems to shut down. In this situation, even the generator wouldn't help. Whatever the case, we were rolling again.

Tip: When traveling in an RV or car, pick out a destination according to approximately how far you want to travel for the day. Be sure to plan to arrive way before dark. Call ahead to see if sites are open and available. Using a cell phone, although aggravating at times, can come in handy. When you arrive at a reasonable hour, you have time to take a walk, get set up, and relax before dinner.

Big Tip: Stop and find a place to stay *before dark*. No matter how eager you are to "make road time," it is not worth the after-dark stress.

Cambridge, Ohio

After leaving Pennsylvania, we stayed at Salt Fork State Park outside of Cambridge, Ohio. The largest State Park in Ohio, it offers boating, hiking trails, and golfing as well as camping on all levels: tenting, trailers, and accommodations for RVs. It is located about 100 miles from Columbus. We wanted to get home to St. Louis. I need to touch home base about every three months, I realized.

On our way home through Effingham, Illinois, we knew we couldn't go through Effingham without seeing Father Tom. We were surrogate parents for Father Tom while he was studying at Kenrick Seminary in St. Louis. He is now a priest of St. Anthony Catholic Church. Luckily, we were able to eat dinner with him. I was telling him about writing this book. My purpose was to help others have the courage to "Run Away From Home After 50." He gave me some profound words of wisdom. (Coming from

*a Man of God, I was not surprised.) He said,
"What you are doing takes the Faith of God.
Do not be afraid to do something different from
what we were accustomed. Be flexible with
Faith and have a heart of adventure."*

That felt very right to me.

*He also said what mankind is doing is
finding our Jerusalem in every place and in every
day of our lives. This really is the thread on which
this book is being written. When you find your
Jerusalem wherever you are, you truly find pure
happiness, peace, excitement, and enthusiasm.
I wish this for everyone who reads this book.
It can be done; we are living it and doing it.*

*I feel very peaceful and happy. There is so
much to see, so many new people to meet, so much
to learn and so much to share. I am excited every
day with anticipation. Life is Good!*

Chapter 13
Repair Woes Back Home

St. Louis, Missouri

We arrived "home" safely and settled into the Casino Queen RV Park in East St. Louis. This new RV park has full hook-ups, cable-TV, phone hook-ups, and great security. It also has a hotel, which is nice for family and friends who might want to stay nearby. Of course, the Casino has become a drawing card for people who like to gamble. People can drive across the river from St. Louis and be there in just a few minutes.

I would recommend the Casino Queen RV Park for anyone visiting St. Louis. With the Metro Link right at the Casino, one can conveniently go to Union Station, Central West End, or the airport. The cost is reasonable at $450.00 for a one-month stay or $24.00 for overnight. You can also get free breakfast buffet coupons worth about $5.95. What a deal! I give the Casino Queen RV Park a Four-Star rating.

We were happy to be home in St. Louis to visit family and friends. We were greeted like celebrities the day we went to our former church. It happened to be my B-Day, too. My son Steve flew in from Denver for the occasion. We saw my daughter's beautiful new home for the first

*time and got lots of hugs and lots of love. That is
all that matters.*

*It was also Thanksgiving—my very favorite
holiday. We have so much to be thankful for.
Thanksgiving ensures we remember how lucky
we are. Our sister-in-law Marilyn and brother-
in-law Dan got the whole family together. We
enjoyed echoes of Love, Love, Love, and Fun.
And the beat goes on.*

Maintaining My Business On The Road

Reflections In Design is an art consulting firm I created 15
years ago. I started it off the "seat of my pants" with one print
catalog, some frame samples, and matte samples. I am now
doing business with MasterCard International, Graybar, The
Nidus Center, G.A. Sullivan Color Art, A.G. Edwards, and
many national and international firms. Lindsey Andrews is
actively running my business while we travel.

I didn't want to give up my business when we started living on the road. Therefore, I believe Lindsey was put into my
life by Divine Order. My husband and I are both so grateful
that we can accomplish this, even while traveling. We had
met a couple parked next to us at the Casino Queen RV Park.
He has his own business doing tattoos while his girlfriend
works at a local nursery school. See what great flexibility you

can have (without the responsibilities of property ownership) when you live in a trailer or RV?

Running a business while traveling takes some creative management and good dependable people. We feel we have created the best of all worlds. And coming home to St. Louis is so much fun because I get to take my clients out to lunch and socialize with them.

Rec Tec and Other Blessings

One Saturday morning, we woke up to find that our Aqua Hot, the system responsible for the heat and hot water was not working. Unfortunately, no repair facility was available for us to call and ask questions on the weekend. So Paul got out The Manual, otherwise known as "The Bible." He did get the heat pump working so we'd have some heat. With little or no hot water, lightning-fast showers were the order of the day.

Monday, we woke up to a "very cool" coach. I said to Paul, "We need to get this coach fixed no matter how much it costs." He called around to see who could fix it immediately. One dealer said there would be a two-week wait for service. Another dealer said his people could possibly work on it the next day. But because the temperature was below freezing, we needed this problem dealt with immediately. Then one dealer recommended a small job shop, Rec Tec off McDonnell Boulevard.

Luck, Divine Order, and all of our angels got together, I'm sure. The people at Rec Tec told us to bring it in and they called the Aqua Hot factory in Colorado to walk them through the problem. After eight hours of having it in pieces, they fixed it. Paul drove the coach home about 6:30 p.m.

We quickly realized that among the most important blessings in our lives are heat, hot water, full hook-ups, and pull-throughs.

See how one's focus changes. Once again, we were in good shape.

Hook-ups: Full Hook-ups include electric, water, and sewer. Full hook-ups are the most desirable but often are not available. When full hook-ups aren't available, partial hook-ups of water and electric are next best. Most campgrounds have a dump station where you can dispose of the sewage.

Pull-throughs: That refers to a campsite at a campground where you can pull your camper or RV completely through the camp site and you don't have to back into the space.

Tip: Repairs on one's coach can be stressful. Having competent people when needed is a must. Rec Tec is a wonderful and dependable RV repair shop in St. Louis. We recommend it highly.

Weather Challenges in December

December in St. Louis. The parts we needed to repair our problems were being shipped to St. Louis, so we had to stay put awhile. Now picture this. The temperature was sub-zero, the wind chill was 25 degrees below zero—not ideal weather conditions when living in a motor coach. Some of the parts that we were waiting for had arrived at Rec Tec so Paul took the coach in. I had spent a busy day in St. Louis and got across the river to E. St. Louis to wait for Paul to return to the RV park. He arrived about 6:30 p.m. I went over to the coach to help him get set up. Then it happened again. No lights, no interior power, and NO CLUE what was causing the problem.

Paul immediately called Rec Tec. Luckily the technicians were still there and waited for us to return to their shop. When we got there, Paul drove our 42-foot motor home into their garage/shop! It barely fit—one more foot and they would not have been able to close the door. They were able to quickly fix the "solonoid," a part that gives no warning when it malfunctions and when it quits, so does everything else.

So we spent the night inside the coach in Rec Tec's garage. We felt comfortable, warm, and safe. Luckily, our problems happened at a place where such willing and knowledgeable technicians could help us.

The next morning, we woke up to eight inches of snow. We went back to the campground determined to get ready and leave St. Louis soon. Mike and Becky Marrs from Soldotna, Alaska, helped Paul chip away the ice on the coach's slide-out. "Everyone helps each other"—a definite ethic in camping or RVing. It is the way the world should always be.

We wanted to be ready to get out of this weather as soon as the last of the parts arrived. The forecast was for 12 to 14 inches of snow. What fun! Thankfully, Fed-Ex came through and delivered the additional parts so we could finally get out of town before more bad weather hit. This is one of the great advantages of our lifestyle. We're never stuck! Well, not for long.

Chapter 14
Heading to Texas

Memphis, Tenn.

Right across the street from Graceland, Elvis's home in Memphis, is an RV park called Memphis/Graceland on Elvis Presley Boulevard. (For reservations call 1-800-562-9386.) We stay there because of its convenient location.

Graceland is a slice out of the past. It has a gate connecting the campground to the Elvis theater, snack bar, and museum. You can watch old Elvis's movies at the theater. The snack bar serves food Elvis loved such as peanut butter and jelly sandwiches and hambergers. A gift shop nearby sells Elvis memorabilia and the Museum houses Elvis's pink Cadillac and other cars and motorcycles. His airplanes include the Lisa Marie and others. They are outfitted with a bed and kitchen just in case he wanted a special peanut butter sandwich in the middle of the night.

The Heartbreak Hotel, which is next to the campground, is distinct because of its throbbing red neon heart on the front of the building.

Across the street is the two-story southern mansion with white pillars—Graceland, where Elvis lived.

We didn't just visit Elvis's place while we were in Memphis. We took lots of time to visit Paul's mom who is 95 years old and an incredible woman. Unfortunately, she had a stroke while we were visiting so we took her to the hospital then located a nursing home for her. Although not exactly what we had planned, we felt grateful we could help her at this critical time.

Lexington, Kentucky

My sister-in-law MaryLou and brother-in-law Ernie own an incredible horse farm in Lexington. Our families gathered there for Christmas, including my son Steven who drove from Denver to be with us all. We appreciate being with our children and especially appreciate our grandchildren Sophia Elizabeth and Samuel Paul, the light of our lives.

The holidays are so magical, yet I sometimes feel overwhelmed with too much of everything: too much sugar, too many conversations, too much sitting around. With the lack of exercise and private time during the holidays, I told myself I must adjust and kept adjusting my focus. It's important to keep readjusting until it feels right to the body, mind, and soul. I know that awareness is the first step to any adjustment. I recommend taking some time for yourself. Stop the busyness. Go to bed early and get plenty of rest. Get a massage and facial. Do nothing except pamper yourself. Completely relax for two days. Gently get back to your routine of exercise and meditation. You will feel just fine again.

Grand Isle, Louisiana

We were heading south on Highway 55 toward New Orleans for New Years but instead by-passed New Orleans and went to Grand Isle, Louisiana, for a few days of peace and quiet. Its population doubles in the summer months, but there's little going on in the winter. The houses there are built on stilts because of hurricanes.

Truly a quiet place, Grand Isle is an island with quiet fishing towns at the tip of Louisiana's south east corner. The temperature there ranges from 30 to 40 degrees in January—not really warm but better than the sub-zero temps we had experienced farther east.

We parked at Grand Isle State Park close to the beach. We found it serene and peaceful on the beach, which was just what we needed. It only costs $3.00 a night and when campers pay for two nights, they get the third night free. What a deal!

We spent a relaxing New Year's Eve eating pizza and raw vegetables. By 8:00 p.m., we were already in bed. After sleeping 12 hours, we felt much better and started the New Year working out. We are committed to staying healthy, therefore we put exercise at the top of our agenda.

Lafayette, Louisiana

We moved on to Lafayette and a campground called Maxies on Interstate 90 on the way to Texas. We belong to an RV club called Passport America, which means we get half off of the regular price of the campground.

Tip: When you join various RV clubs, you can get discounts from participating campgrounds all over the United Sates and Mexico. Good Sams* and KOA* campgrounds give its members a 10% discount while Passport America* gives 50% off the regular price.

In Lafayette, we found a Cajun restaurant nearby recommended by the campground hosts. We enjoyed the good food and lively Cajun music as well as good dancing. Whatever your interests, just ask your campground hosts where to go. They'll answer your questions about the community and its services, so don't be shy to get their recommendations.

Tip: The laundry facilities at Maxies Campground were great. Laundry facilities that are clean are most welcome. You can find what amenities are available at the various campgrounds in the *Woodalls Campground Guide*, definitely the camper's Bible.

* See Organizations to Join in back of this book.

Livingston, Texas

We made it to Livingston, Texas, where we became Real Texans (as the Escapees* call it). This is where we chose to get our car and coach registered, our driver's licenses, and our voter's registrations. Livingston, Texas, became our permanent address because all of our mail comes here through the Escapees mail-forwarding service.

One of the reasons we picked Texas for our residency is because it has no state income tax. In addition to that, the Escapees were recommended to us by other satisfied travelers. We visited Livingston and liked what the campground and the Escapees had to offer. We have been more than pleased with their service and services. We know there are other mail-forwarding services available through the FMCA (Family Motor Coach Association) and others.

Tip: If you establish residency in Texas like we did, be sure to check on the cost of insurance. We found RV Alliance to be less expensive in the state of Texas than other states. The people at the Escapees are a wonderful source of information for all situations. They can answer questions like how to get inspections, registrations, and licenses for your car and coach. We needed to get our hair cut so the Escapees employees recommended Images, a hair salon in Livingston. Gail Smith did a great job.

The Escapee Campground is a safe community with permanent homes as well as trailers and motor homes. It has a Care Center where people who have health challenges can receive care. This unique facility is also a daycare center. The people using the service must be mobile and independent.

Transportation to shopping and lunch gatherings is furnished and activities such as bingo and crafts are available. Laundry service is offered two times a week and trailers are cleaned once a week.

The cost depends on the level of care. Level I is $700.00 per month, which is the highest level of care. The $700.00 includes transportation and activities and $90.00 toward utilities. Meals cost extra.

Level 2 care is $575.00 per month. If additional care is needed, they will help you find people to assist. The Care Center also accepts people who live in town. There is an application that must be filled out and accepted.

People who have RVs and coaches and cannot travel anymore can come to live here in their campers. In fact, others who live here volunteer to look after them.

Since we are Escapee members, the campground fees are reasonable: about $11.00 a day for water and electric hookups. In January, the weather is in the 60s and 70s. For us, it was the first day in months we could go out without our coats. Hooray—finally the weather we had been looking for. It gave us a chance to wash the coach and the car. It had been so long, I had forgotten just what color our coach was.

* See Organizations to Join in back of this book.

Campground Social

While in Livingston, we went to a pancake breakfast— only $2.50 a person for all the pancakes you can eat, sausage, juice, and coffee.

Social activities like these are offered at the various campgrounds and gave us a chance to meet other RVers. This campground is mainly for the members of the Escapees but others can stay for three days to check out the campground before joining the organization.

At this park, we met Livio and Pauline Sandrin and were invited to their place for cappuccino and cookies. They, too, are full-time RVers. It is amusing sharing stories as well as tips. The Sandrin's spend six months in Italy every year and we have been invited to visit them there. Who knows, we may take them up on their invitation.

We have met so many interesting people along the way. I liken RVing to living in Disney World. In Disney World, everyone loves being there. RVers are happy and excited about life because they are doing what they want to do and loving it.

We find RVers go out of their way to be helpful and cheerful. To me, this is the "real world"—the way the world should be, having fun with a sense of adventure. Traveling with this attitude keeps people young and healthy with plenty to look forward to every day. We love it.

Austin, Texas, and Optimum Health Institute

On the way to Austin, we stopped in Houston and spent time with friends. Russell Nees, manager and dean, describes Optimum as a health retreat, but it is so much more. OHI is a Body, Mind, and Spirit experience. It offers informative classes on how to get back to Optimum Health. Russell is a retired minister who is perfect for this place because his experience as a minister brings the spiritually needed for healing. He makes perfect health seem so easy to attain. The staff and instructors are outstanding. So are the massage therapists, chiropractor Dr. Suzie, and colonic therapists Lou Ann, India, and Rasa.

Some people go to Optimum to lose weight; others go to learn how to eat well and prevent health problems down the road. Some already have serious health challenges and go there to heal. The results are miraculous.

I met a man who had two melanomas on his back. The doctors said they were too deep to operate so the man went to Optimum, put himself on the program for six months, and has healed himself.

Mary, the nutritionist at Optimum, had such bad arthritis that she could not open a jar. Coming to Optimum and staying on the program, the mobility in her hands has returned.

OHI can accommodate 25 to 30 people in its small, intimate setting in Austin. It also has a center in San Diego. We had the opportunity to meet wonderful people interested in taking care of themselves. Health is really all that matters; without it, we have nothing.

We have gone to Optimum several times over the years. The program is a three-week program, although people can come for one or two weeks. I recommend staying two weeks on a first visit. Some people make this experience an annual event as we do. When we go, it feels like old home week. (You can learn more at the web site for Optimum Health Institute at www.optimumhealth.org)

We finished a successful week at Optimum and met some wonderful people on their path to health. Jim Beattie, a former professional boxer, was there; a whole family of people suffering from chronic diabetes was there. The healing stories were inspirational. We left feeling we had made many new friends.

San Antonio, Texas

San Antonio has a diverse mixture of cultures and heritages. The River Walk is a fun way to see part of the city; so is going on a river cruise. The Alamo is a famous shrine established to commemorate the site of the famous battle of 1836 for Texas independence.

Fredricksburg, Texas

We stayed at a Good Neighbor Park called Oakwood (with our coupon, it only cost $10.00 a night with full-hook-ups) right in town. Admiral Chester Nimitz, a famous commander of the Navy in World War II, was born in Fredricksburg. His flagship "The Missouri" was the one on which the Japanese surrendered.

Fredricksburg is filled with German heritage, reflected in the shops along Main Street. It is definitely worth a stop. Downtown, we met some friends, Susan and Joe, who live in Kerrwood just 22 miles down Highway 16. Our dinner together at Oak House on Washington Street was delicious. Susan told us lots of people are retiring in Hunt, Texas, where the air is clean and weather desirable. We decided to pass through Hunt and check it out for ourselves.

Big Bend National Park

The highway to Big Bend National Park is surrounded by mountain ranges as well as desert, spectacular canyons, and awesome rock formations. Big Bend covers 801,163 acres and wildlife, plants, and birds are plentiful. Many of these species can be found nowhere else. Some of the activities available at this beautiful national park are hiking, bird watching, river-rafting, rock hounding. The drive from Alpine, Texas, about 79 miles from the Park, was especially breathtaking. Alpine proved to be a good stop; we stocked up on groceries before going in to the Park.

While at the Park, we got reacquainted with a darling couple, about 75 years old, that we'd met in Livingston, Texas. This couple had just started RVing full time. They were having a lot of fun but realized they should have started this adventure sooner. My motto: Don't wait! If the interest moves you, Do It Now!

Our friend said her husband had fallen asleep at the wheel more than once. I recommend that both the husband and wife learn how to drive the rig, just in case of an emergency. You heard the joke about the man who bought his first coach with cruise control. At the scene of the crash, the police officer asked what happened. The driver said he had put the RV on cruise control and went in the back to go to the bathroom.

I can't emphasize enough to avoid driving for long distances. Driving, as we know, can be stressful. It is important to stay alert. Pace yourself. So what if it takes you a day or two longer to get wherever. Remember, you are on vacation.

The Big Bend RV Campground and Motel at Big Bend is nestled in the mountains outside of Big Bend National Park. The weather, in the 60s and 70s, is conducive for hiking and we did a lot of it in the Park, which is about the size of Rhode Island.

When we entered the Park, we got a map showing a list of hikes, the length of each hike, and what to expect so we could choose the ones that best suited our interest and energy level. The Rio Grande River flows through the area and is present in several of the hikes. I advise using walking sticks.

There is no cell phone service here, but pay phones are available. The visitors' center has wonderful books and other items of interest, and the Rangers are pleased to answer questions. When we were there, they featured a promotion to raise money to promote clean air through the sale of personalized license plates with an attractive logo and "Big Bend National Park-Texas" on them. Of course, we had to support the Park and Texas since we are now Texas residents.

Everyone we met there was friendly and eager to chat. We found we had much in common with Mike and Janie from

Boseman, Montana, since we both have Holiday Rambler coaches. It doesn't take much to start a conversation.

Juarez, Mexico

We wanted to see Juarez, but we were told: Do Not Drive Your Car into Mexico. Park your car on the U.S. side and take a bus or other transportation across the border.

Border towns leave a lot to be desired. Over two million people live in Juarez, which is a crowded and expensive place to live. Seeing Juarez really made us appreciate living in the U.S. At the parking lot on the El Paso/Juarez border, we hooked up with a tour guide with a van. He offered to show us around for $25.00 for two hours. We decided to use his service although we could have taken a trolley into Juarez instead. The cost was about the same.

We stopped at a shop that featured Mexican-made leather products, boots, purses, gifts trinkets, etc. Believe it or not, we didn't buy anything. Living in a motor home makes you think twice before you buy anything. There is only so much room. However, we often buy gifts for our grandchildren.

Our driver also showed us some of the nice residential areas in the El Paso Hills, which was quite a contrast from the poor city areas. I enjoy seeing neighborhoods and imagining how people live there.

Chapter 15

New Mexico

Las Cruces, New Mexico

We found the old town of Mesilla, a onetime Mexican village in Las Cruces, fascinating and especially enjoyed the temperate winter climate. I understand this is another desirable city for retirees. Las Cruces has a dry climate, low humidity, and sunshine 70% of the time year round. Sports and recreation are popular. It has many golf courses, tennis courts, and hiking trails. Fishing at Burn Lake and hunting is fun and easily accessible.

We had to leave our coach at an RV dealership in Las Cruces, one that services Holiday Ramblers. We wanted to get a few items fixed while we traveled to Colorado in our Chevy Tahoe. We also decided to give the coach a thorough cleaning before we left. What a project. It's just like cleaning a big house, although it feels great when the job gets finished!

We had to do some creative packing because we planned to be in Colorado skiing (so we'd need winter clothes), then fly to Cozumel, Mexico, to scuba dive (so we'd need summer clothes). We managed to accomplish that, packing our Chevy Tahoe to the gills.

*Our lifestyle during the next few weeks was
quite a change, staying in motels and eating out*

three times a day. We had become so spoiled
having our home with us. But change is good.
We were excited about doing different things
involving travel during that time period.

Through New Mexico

Driving north on Interstate 25 from Las Cruces, New Mexico, to Albuquerque was simply breathtaking, with awesome mountain ranges surrounding us. We stopped at Socorro, New Mexico, and stayed overnight at the Holiday Inn. When we went to the car to get our luggage, we realized Paul had accidentally locked the keys in the car. A very tense moment. Luckily, we had joined AAA Motor Club, which was an important membership in which to invest. So we called AAA and, within one hour, we had our car keys in hand. We spent a relaxing evening, finally.

Tip: Be sure to join AAA Motor Club*. For about $132.00 a year for husband and wife, you can get a RV Plus membership and easily get help if you have emergencies on the road.

* See Organizations to Join in back of this book

Albuquerque, New Mexico

When we left Socorro, we had planned to spend the night in Albuquerque. We drove into the downtown area and realized that most restaurants were closed on a quiet Saturday. We did find a soup and salad buffet and stopped for lunch, then walked around the area. After being approached by people begging for bus fare, we decided we would drive on to Santa Fe, New Mexico. We did not know where we were going to stay there.

Tip: When we joined Coast to Coast, we got a Quest book, which lists participating hotels and resorts in a wide network. With a Quest card, you can get up to 50% off regular prices. A regular membership in Coast to Coast costs $600 but we decided to pay an additional fee of $1300 and join Coast to Coast Deluxe*. The Deluxe membership gives you many opportunities such as guarantees at any Coast to Coast Park, first choice reservations, and a Quest book filled with discounts.

* See Organizations to Join in back of this book

Santa Fe, New Mexico

Continuing north on I25 is an unforgettable landscape. The mountains completely surrounded us. There had been a light snow so the landscape was sprinkled with white. With its breathtaking panoramic view, it didn't seem there could be so much beauty in one area and for so many miles. Have your camera ready; you will be using it a lot.

We stopped at the Information Center outside Santa Fe, which has so much information available just for asking. It's easy to find out about hotels, restaurants, and places of interest as well as entertainment in the area. We discovered a Bed and Breakfast called Pueblo Bonito Inn with a lot of charm. Surprisingly, it had been an apartment complex several years ago. The B & B staff recommended good restaurants and chatted with us about the town. Pueblo Bonito was within walking distance of town and its many galleries. The staff served its guests tea and snacks every afternoon.

I have never been to a city with so many galleries and beautiful shops. We went to the Georgia O'Keefe Museum, conveniently located in the heart of town. The museum displays O'Keefe's work from the beginning of her career up to her death. It also has many of her husband Alfred Stieglitz's photographs. Her style of art changed dramatically as she developed her skills. O'Keefe and Stieglitz lived in a New York apartment for many years. Some of their first works depict what they saw from the windows of their apartment.

Santa Fe is about 7,000 feet in elevation, which makes the temperatures comfortable in the summer. In January, the days are cool but sunny.

We had a busy day checking out the unique galleries. Since I am an art dealer, beautiful art fascinates me.

The artwork in Santa Fe comes from countries all over the world and is made of various media. One can find paintings, sculpture, jewelry, and clothing as well. The workmanship is excellent. As I walked up and down the many streets filled with galleries, I was amazed at the variety of talent. Santa Fe probably has more artwork concentrated in one place than any other city. We spent several days just checking out the galleries. Then we took a ride into the mountains and drove to the ski area just outside of Santa Fe. What a spectacular drive! The ski area has several runs that weren't crowded, a definite plus. We drove around to the other side of Santa Fe, quite a distance altogether, and discovered another art gallery and foundry where bronze sculpture is cast. We found even more beautiful artwork there, including many pieces of hand made furniture and specially woven rugs. The artists combined varied types of wood in each special piece, a beautiful effect. We saw many unusual glass pieces with bright designs and unusual shapes.

Of course, we didn't miss afternoon tea at our B&B, then went for dinner at a wonderful authentic Santa Fe restaurant in the Hotel Santa Fe. Decorated in perfect Southwestern décor, I think this hotel is one of the prettiest places in Santa Fe. I would recommend eating at The Corn Dance Café (in the hotel).

Taos, New Mexico

Just about 70 miles from Santa Fe through spectacular scenery is the old town of Taos. The mountains and canyons en route are a photographer's dream.

Taos is small compared to Santa Fe, but its warmth and friendliness appealed to us. We loved the wonderful handcrafted jewelry and clothing items here. In fact, Paul bought me an awesome sterling silver cuff bracelet. I felt excited to have something to remind me of Taos and also felt grateful to have such a wonderful husband.

We stayed at The Indian Hills Inn, recommended by the people at the Pueblo Bonita B&B in Santa Fe. It seems the best recommendations we have found and enjoyed are from local people. Everyone is eager to help. We did not use our Quest Card, which is not honored by small hotels and B & Bs.

Taos has many museums, art galleries, and cultural events all year long. Since it is also about 8000 feet in elevation, the climate is pleasant in the summer. In the winter, temperatures get up to 60 degree in the day. This special place feels like a family town, which greatly appeals to us.

We heard the skiing in Taos was good so we drove about 45 minutes through incredible mountains and a winding road to Angel Fire Ski Resort. Paul is an accomplished skier and enjoyed skiing the runs at Angel Fire. Best of all, at 65 years old, he could ski for free. What a deal!

After a few hours, Paul decided he had had as much as his legs could stand so we took the circle drive to Red River and Questa and back to Taos. This town continues to surprise us. There is so much to see and do. We found a health food store Cids that carries organic fruits and vegetables, which is important to us. We ate a pleasant dinner at the Appletree, a restaurant just off the main plaza.

The next day, we drove up to Taos Ski Valley, about 15 miles from town and a 9200-foot elevation. It covers 1200 acres and is known for its steep runs. The area continued to enchant us and we understood first-hand why this state is called the Land of Enchantment. Do not miss this exhilarating experience. The ski area is challenging and breathtaking. There are no lift lines, and the ski-in-ski-out accommodations make lodging convenient for skiers. Every kind of food is available, from cafeterias to fine dining. If you are 65 years old or older, a lift ticket only costs $31.00.

Unfortunately, the day we went to Taos Mountain, a winter storm came in and a combination of snow sleet, rain, and high winds made the skiing difficult. So we quickly packed up and headed down the mountain. Luckily, we have a four-wheel-drive car. Although the snow wasn't that deep, we felt safe and secure in our Tahoe.

From the ski resort, we drove to Rio Grand Gorge, which runs right through a valley to the edge of town. This spectacular sight appeared out of nowhere.

The Rio Grand River is the third largest river course in the United States. The first largest river course is the Mississippi, the second being the Missouri. It is a unique river that flows above timberline in Colorado, and flows through the desert. It is fed by tributaries and flows through to New Mexico, through Texas into Big Bend National Park and into the Gulf of Mexico. It is a major flyway for migratory birds.

Every day we spent in this area, we felt its magic. We decided we'd return for a much longer stay.

Take time to open your eyes and see this
beautiful country that God gave to each one of us.
It is up to each of us to see, to explore, and to
enjoy these wonderful gifts. The beauty surrounds
us, putting a smile in our hearts and on our faces.
Enjoy it all. Take time to live life to the fullest.

Chapter 16
Colorado and Cozumel

Salida and Buena Vista, Colorado

We took the scenic drive up Highway 50 and 285 to Salida and Buena Vista. Mountains surround this area for about 150 miles. It looks like it's out of a storybook! It had just snowed and the mountaintops were exquisite. Many of the peaks reach 14,000 feet. We really enjoyed the pristine and peaceful serenity of this area.

We stayed at the Adobe Inn B & B in Buena Vista, right on the main route. It is a charming town, well worth the stop. Nearby are many winter and summer sports opportunities, including skiing, rafting, hiking, golf, mountain biking, and more. We ate good Mexican food at Casa de Sol, right next to the B & B.

Colorado Springs, Colorado

We continued along on our journey to Colorado Springs to visit friends there and drove even more beautiful Colorado mountain passes. The drive from Buena Vista on Highway 24 is a sight to behold. We visited our good friends Jim and Karen Schomaker who invited us to stay with them. We accepted the invitation quickly and gratefully.

The Springs, as it is called, is famous for The Garden of the Gods, a city park with dramatic red rock formations. Here, visitors and citizens love to hike, picnic, ride bikes, even go rock climbing. Located right next to Garden of the Gods is

The Navigators, a missionary organization. It was the estate of William Jackson Palmer, the man who owned the Denver Railroad and developed the city of Colorado Springs in the 1800s. Today, the estate is used for a conference center. Rooms at "The Castle" on the estate can be reserved just like booking a B & B or hotel. It is a very impressive place.

My son, Steven, was a part of the Navigator program several years ago. He worked and lived in The Springs. On this trip, Steven drove down from Denver, met us for lunch, and gave us a tour of Palmer's estate at Glen Eyre. We never could have experienced Glen Eyre if it hadn't been for him. Thanks Steven. We had a great time.

Traveling North

After our Colorado Springs visit, we drove to Denver where some of our children and grandchildren live. What a pleasure and joy to visit our family. We are especially getting to know our Sophia and Samuel better as they grow up. They are so fun!!

After a week with our Denver family, we went to an Elderhostel in Steamboat Springs. Elderhostel is for people over 55 years old. (If you are a couple, only one person has to be 55 years old.)

Tip: Elderhostel* has travel opportunities all over the world and can be accessed on the Internet at www.elderhostel.org. The choices this group offers is endless and costs are extremely reasonable, with meals and lodging usually included. Whether you are single or a couple, it is a great way to meet others of like interests. Elderhostels are located from Antarctica to the South Pole. We keep meeting people who have attended as many as 50 Elderhostels all over the world. Often the people you meet at Elderhostels become good friends.

* See Organizations to Join in back of this book

Steamboat Springs, Colorado

I can't say enough about this sleepy little town. In the winter, of course, if offers dozens of sports opportunities, skiing, snowshoeing, and a lot more. My husband Paul loves skiing. Being a non-skier, I have found many other things to do. We stayed at the Rabbit Ears Motel with the Elderhostel group. The motel is on a historic register and was named for Rabbit Ears Pass. It certainly fills all one's needs.

Driving into Steamboat from the south, you can't miss the pink Rabbit Ears sign! Although it is not fancy, the motel is convenient to everything in town. And if we didn't want to walk, we took a free bus service all over Steamboat.

Steamboat is a great city with all the necessities: massage therapists, a health food store, chiropractors, great restaurants, great shopping, and a wonderful library. Friendly people, too. If you need a chiropractor, massage, facial or acupuncture, I would recommend The Healing Hands on Oak Street. Dr.

Linda Halteman is a wonderful chiropractor and Heidi gave me an incredible facial.

Steamboat is my kind of town and we'll be going back.

Estes Park, Colorado

The drive from Steamboat Springs to Estes Park via Highway 14 is a sight to behold. Its rock formations, canyons, and streams are truly a gift from God. Estes Park, just a few miles from Rocky Mountain National Park, is nestled in the foothills of the mountains. Every angle reveals another spectacular view of the mountains. In the summer, the temperature is about 70 to 80 degrees and it drops at night. The elevation is 6000 feet and the humidity negligible. This area offers many activities for both summer and winter, including hiking, biking, snowshoeing, and cultural events. Not far outside of Estes Park, the YMCA of the Rockies offers many activities as well as accommodations.

In Estes Park, we chose to stay at the historic Stanley Hotel. Built in 1909, it is a classic structure built by F.O. Stanley, one of the brothers who invented a car called the Stanley Steamer. The Stanley Steamer was driven by steam and built at the beginning of the 20th century.

Not only is the hotel classy, elegant, and beautiful, but it also offers top service. The food is excellent and reasonably priced. Kevin leads tours and is in charge of the museum located in the lower lobby of the hotel. The Stanley Hotel is a living history book of the turn-of-the-century events in the Estes Park and Rocky Mountain National Park area. F.O. Stanley was instrumental in developing this area. Kevin does an incredible job of bringing this era to life. He is a history major and he wrote his thesis on the Stanley Hotel and its builder.

We spent four days at the Stanley so we could explore the area and enjoy the beauty of Rocky Mountain National Park. In fact, we were so taken with the area that we applied to be Campground Hosts the next summer, a three-month commitment. We decided it would be a good change of pace.

Cozumel, Mexico

Our plans called for a vacation with our family so we drove to Denver, then flew to Cozumel for almost a week. If you like water, scuba diving, snorkeling, boating, and eating, Cozumel is a perfect getaway place. We stayed at the Plaza Los Glorious, a hotel right on the ocean, convenient to town, and within walking distance to almost everything. Our children and grandchildren loved the beach. Paul and our sons Paul and Steven especially loved the scuba diving while my daughter-in-law Joan and I enjoyed relaxing (if one can relax around two young ones, two-year-old Sophia and four-year-old Sammy).

Many of the commercial cruise ships make Cozumel one of their ports of call because of its beauty and ideal weather. I could sit and look at the intense blue water all day long.

One day, Joan, Paul, Steven, and young
Sammy went fishing for half a day, or so they
thought. Their boat broke down several times,
which made it frustrating for everyone. About
four hours into the trip, Paul did catch an ahi

tunafish. Sammy was so excited. He was clapping as Paul reeled in the fish. They almost lost the fish but the Mexican crew helped recover the catch and reeled it in. After catching this ahi, they kept trying for more. Everyone was so tired, to say the least. What started out as a half-day excursion turned into an eight-hour adventure. Happily, the ahi was enough for two dinners for seven of us. The hotel prepared it on the grill, and we enjoyed the fish and all the trimmings. Everyone ate very well.

Across from the hotel Plaza Los Glorious is a modern convenience/grocery store that stocks everything imaginable. The food in Cozumel is delicious, well prepared, and reasonably priced. Santiago's restaurant is a favorite of ours (we usually get grilled shrimp) and Prime restaurant is another of our favorites.

Back Home

We felt eager to get back home to our own bed. There is no place like home. After all, we had been gone for six weeks. So we drove back to Las Cruces, New Mexico, where we had left our home. Everything in the coach seemed to check out fine, at first. We found the service at American RV Dealers to be great. The people there were conscientious and willing to listen—a rarity in the RV business.

Driving about 30 miles away from Las Cruces, we kept hearing a loud noise. The wind was fierce, but the noise was louder than we thought it should be. So we pulled off the highway and Paul inspected the front of the coach where the noise was coming from. He noticed a gap in the windshield. Because the wind was so strong, it made the noise even more obvious. We couldn't drive with a problem like this, so we turned around and went back to American RV to get the windshield fixed.

Sometimes problems with the coach can be very frustrating. But I knew that these mechanics would get it right, whatever it took. To solve the problem, they stayed in close communication with the factory in Oregon.

Tip: Don't ever be in too much of a hurry, especially when repairs are needed. That just makes the frustrations greater.

We discovered the windshield wasn't the only problem. Our new satellite dish, which is mounted on the roof of the coach, also caused some frustrating moments. Evidently, the dish was locking in on the wrong satellite. The technician tried everything he knew. He communicated with the satellite dish company and still had no luck. He ended up replacing the receiver. After spending five days in Las Cruces at American RV waiting for the repaired windshield to cure (the technician said it had to "set up" for a certain length of time), we left for Arizona.

If we had not been at the RV dealer getting the window repaired, we would have been beside ourselves with the satellite dish reception problem. So when all is said and done, it worked out well that we had to stay in Las Cruces a few more days. Patience is required when one lives in an RV.

Tip: Did I mention that patience is a virtue? Sometimes you have to find lots of it before you can continue your journey.

Chapter 17
Arizona, California, Nevada

Huachuca City, Arizona

Our campground in Huachuca City (about 40 miles southeast of Tucson) is called The Caverns, a Coast to Coast affiliate that cost only $6.00 a night. It was our home park when we first joined Coast to Coast. Being our home park means we get to stay there for two weeks at no charge.

Travel Home to St. Louis

As Paul settled into the RV park, I flew from Phoenix, Arizona, to St. Louis to spend time with family and friends, and take care of business. I would recommend a visit to St. Louis for anyone, especially in the spring or fall. It is a fun city with lots to see and do: Missouri Botanical Garden, Zoo, Art Museum, St. Louis Symphony at Powell Symphony Hall, Fox (live theater), Repertory Theater (live theater), and The Muny (outdoor live theater in the summer). It has many fine restaurants. St. Louis is an easy city in which to get around. Of course, the Gateway Arch at the Riverfront is a must see.

*It is important for me to follow my heart
and touch home base every three months. I
recommend following your heart, too, whatever*

it may tell you. I spent a whirlwind week in St. Louis visiting family and friends. Everyone was so happy to see me. What an ego trip!

Back to Arizona

The next town from where we parked in Huachuca City is Sierra Vista, about 10 miles away. It has all the conveniences one might need. Tombstone, the Wyatt Earp stomping grounds and cowboy town, is close by. The days are warm and the nights are cool. With no humidity, the weather is perfect for hiking, biking, walking, and just being outside.

Tombstone is a popular destination for RVers. In 1879, the Earps arrived in Tombstone and planned to make a lot of money. It is an authentic Old West trading post built on Wyatt Earp's original mine claim. Silver was discovered here. The town grew by leaps and bounds as people came to mine silver. At one time, the town had 110 licensed drinking establishments. The red light district of Tombstone was bigger than in other towns of its size and even the cemetery "Boot Hill Graveyard" saw more business than towns of its size and population. Tombstone is known as "The Town Too Tough To Die." Wyatt Earp is Tombstone's most famous law enforcement officer as noted by his involvement in the Gunfight at the OK Corral. He resided in Tombstone for about 22 months.

Tombstone takes great pride in its efforts to preserve the past. Reenactments of the Gunfight at the OK Coral can be seen as you walk the streets. The Crystal Palace Saloon and

Big Nose Kate's Saloon were common hangouts for Wyatt Earp, Doc Holiday, and Bat Masterson. Even the bullet holes have been preserved.

Tip: If you need any biking stuff or repairs on any bicycle items, Sun and Spokes in Sierra Vista is a reliable bike shop.

Nogales, Arizona

For a one-day excursion, Nogales is just 50 miles south from Huachuca City on the Mexican border. There, you can walk across the border from Nogales, Arizona, into Nogales, Mexico, where you can buy many things. Do stop at the Visitor Information Center for tips on where to park your car before you walk across the border to Mexico. The staff there will also recommend restaurants on both sides of the border.

Phoenix, Arizona

We took a day's trip to Phoenix, the capital of Arizona. With its many suburbs, Phoenix is growing by leaps and bounds and has everything anyone could want or need including beautiful shops, outstanding resorts, and great restaurants.

If you are traveling in an RV, I recommend staying in Tempe where there is a good campground on Apache Road and McClintock, close to Scottsdale. McClintock Road turns into Hayden. Hayden is a main street with lots of activity that can be enjoyed. We found the Apache Palms RV Park to be well kept and the owners helpful. March and April is an ideal time to visit the area.

The Boyce Thompson Arboretum is a very beautiful place to visit. On Highway 60, it's about 50 miles east from the Scottsdale area and has lots of hiking trails. We especially liked learning about the desert plants and landscaping while we were there.

Quartzsite, Arizona

This is the home of flea markets in the winter, yet by April *everything* closes up. The vendors as well as the snowbirds simply leave. Thousands of RVs dry camp in the winter. Dry camping means there are no hook-ups. I hear the gathering of thousands of rigs in one place is quite a sight.

The town is busy all winter because of the mild temperature. Beginning in October through to March, nine major gem, mineral, and more than 15 general swapmeeting shows are reasons so many RVers come to Quartzsite. The Bureau of Land Management and law enforcement agencies estimate more than 1.5 million people attend these events.

There are approximately 10 RV parks in the area. Many RVers come to boondock (camp in an open field with no hook-ups). When their holding tanks are full, they go and stay at a campground for two to three nights, then go back to boondocking.

Indio, California

Going west from Quartzsite, Arizona into California, we stayed at the Indian Waters Campground in Indio and found it to be one of the best campgrounds we have experienced. Its spacious campsites are surrounded by trees, grass, and flowers.

This campground is close to both Palm Desert and Palm Springs. The weather is in the 70s and 80s in the day; the nights are cool. I would rate it as a four-star campground.

Besides being conveniently located, there are many activities to get involved in. You can even volunteer to work in the campground or at the front desk. When you volunteer at a campground, you usually get a free campsite.

Palm Desert and Palm Springs

Driving west on Highway 111 takes travelers to Palm Desert, which has flowers everywhere and dramatic architecture. We really liked exploring a street called El Paseo, similar to Rodeo Drive in Beverly Hills, California. To see beautiful and unusual things, spend an evening walking down El Paseo Road.

Tip: On Saturdays and Sundays at the College of the Desert in Palm Desert from 9:00 a.m. to 2:00 p.m. is an outdoor festival. You can buy everything you ever desired, from artwork to golf balls to sunglasses to produce at a farmer's market full of vegetables.

The weather is perfect in the winter months, although it gets incredibly hot in the summer. Palm Springs weather ranges from 56 degrees to 89 degrees. January, February, and March have the most pleasant temperatures. Since the area is in the desert, the temperature, although a dry heat, can climb into the 100s in the summer months.

Continuing on Highway 111 is Palm Springs where streets are named after movie stars: Fred Waring Boulevard, Frank Sinatra Boulevard, etc. There are restaurants galore! The winter weather makes it easy to be outside dining, biking, or walking. No wonder the area is so popular for visitors. We noticed a path used for biking and walking on either side of Highway

111. The path goes through Palm Desert, Indian Wells, and parts of Palm Springs.

Tip: While at the Indian Waters campground, we were introduced to another campground organization called Western Horizons*. We investigated the opportunities it offers and decided we would get our money's worth in one to one-and-a-half years. After joining the Western Horizon group, we found out that parking in many campgrounds in the network is available at no charge. The parks are very well kept. Do investigate this opportunity if you are going to spend several months a year in your RV. It is an even more appealing opportunity if you are going to live full time in your RV.

Los Angeles, California

Pyramid Lake Campground is a Western Horizon park nestled in the mountains about one hour north of Los Angeles. It is right off Highway 5, just south of Gorman. Pyramid Lake Campground is also about 45 minutes north of San Clarita on Highway 5. San Clarita is one place you can park your car and take the Metro into L.A. Station. Amtrak trains are available out of the L.A. Station. Universal City Walk and Universal Studios are among many fun places to visit nearby.

We found Amtrak was a good way to get around to Anaheim (Disneyland), San Diego, etc. Since the traffic in and around L.A. is heavy (to say the least), be sure to check out alternate ways to get around.

We had a great time in the L.A. area visiting friends and family we hadn't seen in ages. Walking is a must to keep in shape while on the road. It is easy to do anywhere, even if you only walk around the campground. We have been attending some breakfasts and dinners provided by the campground. The cost is nominal and it also gives us a chance to meet other campers, trade stories, and have fun.

One place of interest in the L.A. area is The Getty, a foundation started by J. Paul Getty. The complex itself is an architectural work of art. It houses museums and spectacular gardens not to be missed. The setting of The Getty is unbelievably beautiful. The Getty is an educational facility where workshops are given to learn about architecture, archeology, and art. You can also take the train ride to Sepulveda where you can see the structure from the top of the hill. Richard Meier is the architect who combined glass and metal to give the contemporary feeling to the structure. The gardens especially are a joy to behold with waterfalls and walking paths and many unusual species of flowers and plants. Don't forget your camera. Be sure to connect with one of the tours to understand the history and the background of this architectural marvel.

Boron, California

On the way to Las Vegas from L.A. is a small town called Boron, California. It has nothing but a boron mine and a museum so I was skeptical about the value of stopping there. But after we pulled into the RV park, we decided to take a walk and found the town's history well worth the stop. Boron is a mineral used in many products. The museum in Boron is extremely educational.

In 1881, Colmanite, a low grade of borax, was discovered in Death Valley. Originally, the mine was owned by the Pacific Coast Borax Company. For five years, beginning in 1883, a wagon train 160 feet long and pulled by 20 mules carried twelve tons of borax from Death Valley to the Mohave Desert where there was a smelter. It took them 20 days.

The mine at Boron, originally named Margo, has been operational since 1913.

Borax was used in Egyptian and Babylonian times. Some of its uses are 20 Mule Team Borax soap, motor oil, transmission fluid, glazes for dishes and cups, polish, footballs, and even playdough.

Las Vegas, Nevada

Las Vegas is definitely a city like no other. The Strip is something to behold. Las Vegas features first class gambling casinos, elaborate hotels, golf courses, gourmet restaurants, fashionable shops, and big name entertainment. The strip is where most of the casinos and hotels can be found. Every place is lit up with bright signs flashing the name of the establishment. The lights are so bright, you don't know if it is day or night.

The hotels are something out of this world and feature lots of good entertainment. The food is reasonably priced, usually, as is the lodging. Of course there is gambling on all levels, if that is your interest. Lake Mead and Hoover Dam are nearby. They are definitely worth a side trip.

We stayed at a Coast to Coast RV Park, Hacienda Adventure Club at Destiny's Oasis Las Vegas Resort. It is a luxurious park with two swimming pools, spas, waterfalls, and an 18-hole putting course. It also offers shuttle service to The Strip. There are many other RV parks in Las Vegas, but we are glad we stayed where we did.

I had an experience that I wish on no one. In California, I got a bad cold that turned into a sinus infection. I was trying to be my own doctor but I just got sicker and sicker. In Las Vegas, I went to an emergency room at one of the hospitals to get some antibiotics—or so I thought. Wrong!!! I was admitted and they diagnosed pneumonia, big time. Doctors kept me in the hospital for four days. They wanted me to stay longer but I promised to be good if they would let me go home. I had to have IV fluids and breathing treatments around the clock. Seriously, I have never been so sick, ever.

I mention this because there is always a chance of getting sick on or off the road. The Desert Springs Hospital in Las Vegas is excellent, although I hope you never have to find out first-hand. Almost every city has wonderful health care facilities with walk-in clinics and, of course, there are emergency rooms at the hospitals. If you "think" you are getting sick, don't wait like I did. Get some help.

Tip: It is **very** important to have health insurance, whether you are an RVer or not. Our primary provider is Medicare. Whomever is your primary provider becomes your secondary provider as soon as you become eligible for Medicare at 65. The rates will drop when you go on Medicare.

Be sure you have your health insurance paid up because the last thing you want to happen is to become ill and not have health insurance. Your health insurance should cover you wherever you might get sick. Check with your insurance company to make sure, especially if you subscribe to an HMO.

Colorado

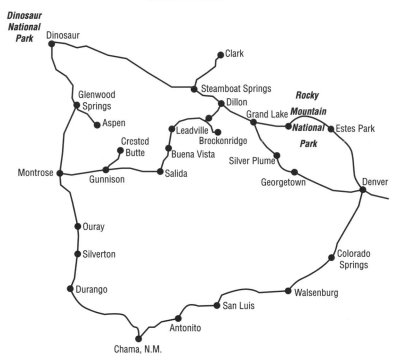

Chapter 18
Camp Hosts and Colorado Adventures

Estes Park, Colorado

Estes Park is a beautiful town about two hours drive northwest of Denver. The elevation is about 8500 feet. The temperature is cool in the summer with no humidity. Rocky Mountain National Park is just outside of Estes Park where there's a lot to do: hiking, biking, floating, fishing, camping, relaxing, and much more.

Rocky Mountain National Park has several campgrounds in and around it, including four inside the Park. On the Estes Park side are Glacier Basin and Moraine Park campgrounds, which both require reservations. On the Grand Lake side of the mountain is a first-come-first-serve campground called Timber Creek.

Be sure to call and make reservations early in the season because sites do fill up quickly, especially in the summer. You can pay for your reservations with a credit card. Just call Destinet 1-800 365 CAMP (365-2267) to reserve sites up to five months in advance.

Campground Hosts at Rocky Mountain National Park

When we became campground hosts, the woman in charge of volunteers at Rocky Mountain National Park was very helpful. Our friendship with her has become special to us. As campground hosts, we got no monetary pay but we did get our campsite with full hook-ups for free. It gave us a beautiful place to live nestled among the trees and looking at the glaciers every day. We were excited to stay put for a few months at Glacier Basin.

Campground Hosts' Job Description

Our job as campground hosts consisted of checking campers into appropriately sized campsites. Of course, tents would use smaller sites while large RVs would need much more space.

Glacier Basin campground has 150 sites, which we found to be quite manageable. Moraine Park has 250 sites and can get very noisy. Mostly our duties included keeping campers happy. We assigned campsites, informed campers of park rules, and answered questions of all varieties. We also checked campsites for possible bear problems. Leaving food outside a vehicle can be a serious problem. Both bears and campers must be educated about proper food storage. Because bears have an incredible sense of smell that reaches more than 50 feet, shampoo, toothpaste, and anything with an odor must be properly stored.

We also assisted the Rangers, who are paid personnel, in any way we could as "park ambassadors." This was right up our alley because both Paul and I really love people.

As campground hosts, we worked four days a week and took off three. We were also given a day every other week to explore Rocky Mountain National Park. We wore uniforms when we went hiking and talked to visitors along the way. People were always asking questions. Usually we could answer them, but sometimes we had to find out the answers from the Rangers. We loved those educational days on the trail! In case we ran into any problems, we had a radio to report any situations in which people needed assistance.

We also had some tense situations to deal with.

Early one evening as we were getting off duty, two young women ran, horrified, to our campsite. They had been cooking dinner and saw a bear come into their campsite. It turned out they were Girl Scout leaders who had taken the girls for a hike earlier in the day. Two of the girls had left candy in their backpacks, which had been left in their tents. The bear smelled the candy (their sense of smell is very sharp). Bears that season were especially hungry because they had not been able to get enough food during the previous spring. It had been a dry season and they usually feed on berries.

The bear slashed open the girls' tent, grabbed the backpack, and went off to tear it open and see what he could find to eat. Luckily the girls had not been in the tent and no one was hurt.

However, the bear returned when the Scouts were fixing dinner. Everyone went hysterical! Paul walked over to their campsite to see what he could do. We also called Dispatch to report the bear sighting. Dispatch is a central communication station in Rocky Mountain National Park. Dispatch can locate help for problems happening in the park. Park Rangers and Security carry radios so they can be reached day or night. Campground hosts also carry radios for reporting problems. Dispatch radioed the rangers who came over to the scene as soon as possible. The girls stayed in their leaders' vans until the bear could be coaxed to leave the scene.

The leaders apologized repeatedly. They had not made it clear to the girls the importance of not leaving anything edible in their tents. It proved that, usually, bear problems were caused by humans; bears just want to feed themselves.

I am sure the Girl Scouts will never forget this incident. Nor will we! Campground hosts have the critical responsibility to inform campers of the rules and the dangers that could possibly come up while they are having fun.

Fun While We Work

As campground hosts, we met people from all over the world, including couples from the United Kingdom and Germany. I really believe this job is about being Good Will Ambassadors for the National Park as well as for our country.

Mary Lou and Ralph Feldt, the couple we worked with and the other campground hosts at Glacier Basin, were from Michigan. They had been full-time RVing for five years and have been campground hosts at other National Parks. They just love their life. The Rangers—Diane, Jerome, Janette, and Vicki—came from all walks of life and decided to experience a Ranger lifestyle for a while.

Trail Ridge Road

Just 50 miles from the Headquarters entrance of Rocky Mountain National Park is the town of Grand Lake. Between the two points, the drive across Trail Ridge Road is unbelievably spectacular. It actually takes about two-and-one-half hours each way through alpine terrain to travel those 50 miles, but it is well worth it. Snow closes the road frequently, so check weather conditions before starting out on Trail Ridge Road. Be sure to stop at the Alpine Visitors' Center at the top.

Back to Optimum Health Institute

Since I had been ill and was recovering from pneumonia, I opted to return to Optimum to restore my health and energy. I know this is "my place" to regain my health. I sensed that the antibiotics that I had needed to save my life left a residue in my intestines. This results in fatigue.

I want to emphasize what a great retreat Optimum is for healing and resting. We consistently eat "live" food including wheat grass and raw foods. All meals are prepared as part of the weekly fee.

People from all over the world go to OHI in San Diego or Austin to get healed. The facility was built by Cory Carson, Johnny Carson's son. The word is out and Optimum has a waiting list most of the time. It features a pool, a hot tub, and a walking path, yoga classes, water aerobics and much more. If you want to learn how to take care of your health on any level, experience Optimum. Because it is a non-profit organization, it is reasonably priced (see www.optimumhealthinstitute.org).

I have been back several times to Optimum and am feeling better and better. My energy, my health, and my spirit are always rejuvenated. I am so very grateful for this place.

Our grandchildren Sophia Elizabeth and Samuel Paul live in Denver with their parents Joan and Paul. Being in the Rockies and so close to Denver, we got to see our children and grandchildren often. Our other son, Steven, also lives in Denver. Sammy and Sophie have called me Black Grandma for many years because I have dark hair. They were trying to keep me separate from their Grandma Connie who has blonde hair. They call her White Grandma. One day

when I called our children's home, Sophie
answered the phone. She proceeded to run and
tell her Mom (in the shower at the time) that
Grandma In the Woods was on the phone.
I like my new name much better.

Grand Lake, Colorado

When we left our volunteer position, we continued to explore the area and decided to go to Grand Lake via Trail Ridge Road. It is one of the longest expanses of scenic highway in the U.S. that crosses the Continental Divide. We camped at Timber Creek, a first-come first-serve campground with 100 sites and no hook-ups. This charming campground is definitely "in the woods." The fees here and at other Park campgrounds were $16.00 a night. (If you are 62 years old or older, don't forget your Golden Age Pass to get a savings.)

There, we got together with friends we met in Arizona, Gary and Eileen Shapiro and Marcia and Irv Solomon. They were also roaming the U.S. We agreed we are all enjoying this wonderful life of freedom and fun.

The Grand Lake Lodge is a must see in Grand Lake. The porch at the lodge overlooks Grand Lake and is known as the Favorite Porch in Colorado because of the view. At least the Grand Lake Lodge says so.

Grand Lake has lots of water sports and places to rent boats of all sorts. It has small sandy beach and access to lots of hiking trails on the east side of the Park.

The town of Grand Lake also has a Repertory Theater that is fabulous. The summer Rep draws a great caliber of artists from all over the world. We saw "Hello Dolly" there. Be sure to check out the Rep.

Steamboat Springs, Colorado

Steamboat Springs is both a great ski town in the winter and a wonderful town in the summer. This time, we stayed at the KOA campground just a few miles out of town. Since our skiing trip to Steamboat in the winter, I had become familiar with the town. I especially loved the Mad Creek Gallery in town, which carries original paintings and may be branching out into photography.

I also discovered another place to get massages, facials, body wraps: Rocky Mountain Spa. It is out by Mount Werner and the Steamboat Grand Resort on Burgess Creek Road.

We checked out several golf courses including the Sheraton Steamboat, which is a challenging and beautiful course. The Yacht Club is a great restaurant on the Yampa River right in town. Don't miss the bookstore and café just off 7th Street. Fish Creek Falls is beautiful and is just a few miles out of town. (Take Third Street by the post office and follow the signs.) We also learned about Strawberry Park, a beautiful hot springs experience just out of town.

Steamboat Lake, about 20 miles out of town on Highway 129, has lots of camping and boating. Be sure to make reservations early; it is popular and the park fills up quickly in the summer. (For reservations call 970-879-3922.)

I found some great shops in Steamboat, in particular, a wonderful children's shop called Steamboat Kids. It is worth stopping in if you are in the market for unusual children's clothing. Healthy Solutions on Lincoln and Third Street is a great health food store next door to the Rabbit Ears Motel. It stocks everything you might need to keep you healthy as well as provides great lunches.

Our friends Kelli, Steve, and Maddy King live in Clark, just a few miles out of Steamboat. They work at the Vista Verde Ranch, which offers a wealth of both winter and summer activities for their guests. Kelli and Steve are available to lead hiking, biking, snowshoeing and other activities.

Other friends Linda and Perry Blankenbiller flew up from St. Louis to visit with us in Steamboat for a few days. We feel so blessed having such wonderful friends that we get to connect with along our travels.

Dinosaur National Monument

Driving west from Steamboat Springs, we took Highway 40 west to Highway 64 and went to Dinosaur, Colorado, about 130 miles from Steamboat. Our campground there honored discounts for Good Neighbor and Coast to Coast members so the charge was only $10.00 a night.

The big attraction is taking the shuttle to the Dinosaur Quarry—a spectacular place. The Quarry was established as a National Monument in 1915 by Woodrow Wilson. About 50 years later, Franklin D. Roosevelt expanded the Monument's boundaries. The quarry, where actual dinosaur bones were found, has been enclosed and became part of the Dinosaur National Monument.

Going here is definitely a step back in time and well worth planning a vacation around. Within the Monument are miles and miles of scenic drives on the east side. In fact, the distance is about 62 miles round trip to Harpers Corner Road from the parking lot and can take four hours to drive.

In my opinion, this area is even more spectacular than the Grand Canyon. It was certainly an educational trip for our whole family. After my grandson Sammy and his family visited Dinosaur National Monument with us, four-year-old Sammy really got hooked on dinosaurs.

People of all ages will love the Monument for the nearby camping, hiking, and rafting. The Greer River and the Yampa River run through the Park. The rock formations are beyond anyone's imagination.

Aspen, Colorado

It is a beautiful drive from Dinosaur to Aspen along Highway 64, east on Highway 70 through Glenwood Springs, and south on Highway 82 through Basalt to Aspen. We stayed at the Aspen Basalt Campground, about 20 miles north of Aspen. Basalt is the only campground in the area. Don't forget to call ahead for reservations (970-927-3405), especially if you are traveling in the summer.

Aspen is beautiful in the summer and in the winter. If you want to buy property in the area, bring several checkbooks. The property in and around Aspen starts in the millions.

Just for fun, we went to see the historic, restored Jerome Hotel on the main street in Aspen. Paul had skied Aspen in the '50s and '60s when the cost of a room at the Jerome was about $12.00. Imagine what it is today! The Jerome Hotel, a landmark in Aspen, is beautiful and elegant. The Crystal Palace is a dinner theater and has good entertainment. The Aspen Music Festival is a "must see and hear" if you enjoy music.

We were sitting in the lobby of the Jerome Hotel, resting after a walking tour of the town, and started talking to Anna and Stephen Creal from Fort Collins. We were having so much fun chatting that we decided to have dinner together. The Creals are dentists, so if you need dental care and are in or near Fort Collins, they will take good care of you.

The food at the Jerome is first rate and the evening was a wonderful success. Anna's family joined us and, by the end of the evening, we felt like we had known each other forever.

One day we took Highway 82 from Basalt to Aspen. The highway that goes through town goes to Independence Pass and the Continental Divide. If you keep going, you reach

Leadville. Its beauty is well worth the drive. The summer is the ideal time to make this drive because Independence Pass is closed in the winter.

From June until the middle of August, Aspen is famous for the Aspen Music Festival. Students from all over the world apply and must be accepted to play in the various orchestras that play in the summer school. Famous artists join the Music Festival as well. Many of the concerts are free. We attended a concert performed by the students. The quality of music is outstanding.

Tip: If you are in or near Aspen in the summer, don't miss the Music Festival. You will never forget the concerts in the Big Tent because the acoustics in the mountains are superb!

One day, we took a ride to the Maroon Bells, a popular hiking area around Aspen. Buses go up to the area in the daytime because cars are not allowed. After 5:00 p.m., you can drive the road to see some spectacular mountains and scenery.

Breckenridge, Colorado

Breckenridge is a busy town in the summer and winter. Of course, being a ski town, it is a desirable place to live if you can afford the real estate. The nights are cool and the days are warm. The town of Breckenridge is typical of ski towns with its shops and restaurants. There are lots of bicycle riders in this town. One paved bike path even goes from Breckenridge to Frisco.

We parked our coach in a friend's driveway for a few days but scouted out Tiger Run, a large RV Park in Breckenridge, for future reference.

We were invited to Lynn Montgomery's and Tim Hollaman's wedding in Golden, Colorado. We have been long-time friends of Francis and Elsie Montgomery, parents of the bride and also from St. Louis. I feel there is no coincidence that we are in Colorado at the perfect time. We are so happy we could help the family celebrate this outstanding event. Everyone had a great time.

Carol Beth True, a friend for many years, plays music with my cousin Sandy Weltman, also a fine musician. They were in Denver attending the Harmonica Convention when we were there. They are both from St. Louis and performing at a concert in Denver the very weekend we were there. My son Steven, who stays in touch with Sandy, found out about the concert. Sandy got us tickets and we enjoyed a wonderful evening.

The weekend was so full of fun and love. Of course, seeing our children and grandchildren Sammy and Sophie puts the frosting on any cake. Wow! What a weekend.

New Friends in Breckenridge

We went back to Breckenridge to our coach parked in our friend's driveway. As we were taking a walk, we met a man walking his dog, a golden retriever. We love "goldens" so we started chatting. It turns out Tom and Julie Brown, originally from St. Louis, own a wonderful second home in Breckenridge. They live primarily in Texas. Of course, being the friendly guy he is, Tom took us on a tour of their lovely home. We enjoyed meeting Julie, too. Their home actually sleeps 13 people, winter or summer, and can be used for reunions and other special occasions.

Gunnison, Colorado

From Breckenridge, we traveled to Gunnison where we stayed at a Western Horizon Park called Blue Mesa, about 12 miles west of town on Highway 50. The landscape, mountains, and jagged rock are breathtaking. The temperature in Gunnison is in the 60s and 70s in the day but really cools off at night. Since we visited in mid-August, we felt we were in one of the most pleasant places in the country weather wise.

Again, we connected with our friends Eileen and Gary Shapiro, whom we met in Tempe, Arizona, last winter. We stayed in Gunnison with them for three days. They are so fun and funny. We ate dinner together at our coach and

*they brought their own food, making entertain-
ing really easy.*

Buena Vista, Colorado

We stayed at Snowy Peaks RV Park just north of town. There
is wonderful hiking and biking trails as well as skiing nearby.
Buena Vista had become home to our dear friends Karen and
Jim Schomaker since we last traveled in Colorado. The cost of
real estate is comparatively reasonable here compared with other
ski towns in the state. Jim and Karen just bought a wonderful
house that shows off the landscape from every window. They
love their new home and we know why. Their children live in
Colorado so that makes them even happier.

Leadville, Colorado

With Jim and Karen, we took a day trip to Leadville, about
30 miles from Buena Vista. We decided to do a bike ride along
Leadville's newly paved bike trail, which was 12 miles round trip.

Everything started off just fine. I had not been on a bike
in quite a while, so the 12 miles at 10,000-foot altitude really
challenged me. In the course of the uphill ride, we encountered a rainstorm. The rain turned into sleet. Unfortunately,
we were not prepared for the change in the weather and did a
lot of stopping along the way to rest. The 12 miles seemed
extremely long. When we finally reached the cars, we were all
wet, cold, tired, and very happy to be back. We jumped into
our cars and turned on the heat.

Anyway, we had a fun time, as we always do, with Karen and Jim. We ate lunch at The Leadville Brewery. I now own a warm shirt from the Brewery. If they sold trousers, I would have bought those, too.

Tip: After the fact, I can give lots of advice. Here it is: Be sure to bring a jacket and a change of clothes when biking or hiking in the mountains. Rain, snow, and hailstorms are common after 12:00 noon.

Vail, Colorado

Vail is about 30 minutes drive from Frisco along Interstate 70. Vail is an experience in itself. In the summer, the whole town is filled with flowers. It is easy to walk around town but if you wish, you can take free buses everywhere and they run year round.

Vail is a much different experience in the winter than in the summer. The skiing is among the best anywhere and the town has something of everything to tickle your fancy.

There are no RV parks in Vail itself so RVers have to find a campground outside and drive into town. Frisco would be a good place to stop in the summer. However, campgrounds are often closed after Labor Day so check with the White River National Forest (970-468-5400).

While in Frisco, it snowed about four inches in September. As travelers there know, the weather in the mountains is unpredictable. This is when we had a problem with our furnace again. The Aqua Hot, which runs the furnace, just quit working. Consequently, the temperature in the coach was only in the 30s. We went to bed knowing we'd be fine under the covers and hoped for a miracle in the morning.

The next morning, we still had no luck with the furnace. At least the heat pump, which is our auxiliary heat system, did work. Thank God! Finally, the coach warmed up. We put on extra clothes, which helped a lot. We decided to drive to Denver, about two hours away, because it is at a lower elevation and would be warmer than Frisco. We stayed at Denver North Campground. Fortunately, the Aqua Hot factory is in Fort Lupton, Colorado, not far from our campground, and got an appointment quickly. Still another miracle!

On September 11, 2001, we were in Denver when the Disaster happened in New York. Terrorists hijacked four planes. Two planes hit and destroyed the twin towers of the World Trade Center in New York. The third plane hit the Pentagon. The fourth plane, thought to be heading for Washington, crashed in Pennsylvania near Pittsburgh.

THE WORLD STOOD STILL. The Act of War by the terrorists paralyzed every person in the U.S. and probably every person in the world. The president of the United States and the leaders of the world must decide what we must do now. The World Will Never Be The Same!

For us, it became hard to go on with life. All we could do was listen to the happenings on TV or radio. Everyone around us was glued to the TV, compelled to listen to every detail of the horrible event. It is the worst tragedy the United States and the world has ever experienced since World War II.

I felt so sick to my stomach, I could hardly function. Nothing really mattered when thousands of innocent people got killed unnecessarily. No one will ever be the same. We all felt so helpless. Getting back to life will not be easy—for anyone. There are so many questions and so few answers.

Georgetown, Colorado

We had planned to go on an Elderhostel train ride on the narrow gauge railroads all around the state. But due to the Disaster, the trip was cancelled. Of course, we were disappointed but in contrast to the happenings of the last two days, our disappointment was not even an issue.

Even with heavy hearts and stomachs, we decided to go on the train experience ourselves. We left Denver on September 12th and drove to Georgetown, Colorado, about an hour west of Denver. Georgetown is a small town filled with Victorian houses, lots of galleries, wonderful shops, and restaurants. We stayed at the Georgetown Motor Inn and ate dinner at Tasso's Bistro, located next to the Motor Inn.

The train ride on the Georgetown Loop Narrow Gauge Railroad takes about an hour. We boarded it at Silver Plume, the next town just west of Georgetown. Silver Plume is a small town established in the late 1800s and gave us a look at "the way things were then."

The scenery along the route was outstanding and the train ride was a lot of fun. I would highly recommend it.

We left Georgetown and drove west along Interstate 70 to Glenwood Springs. We drove through Glenwood Canyon on the way to the city where we took a dip at the famous Glenwood Hot Springs, close to the historic Hotel Colorado.

Ouray, Colorado

A few hours drive from Glenwood is Ouray, in the southwest corner of Colorado. The ski town of Telluride is close by. The drive to Ouray was another spectacular experience. We enjoyed the town, its restaurants and galleries. The weather is wonderful in the summer, with no humidity. The Indian tribe led by Chief Ouray lived in that area. Miners built and settled the town. It is a popular place for those who like to ride up the mountains in jeeps. There are 700 miles of jeep trails. Although the town is surrounded by mountains, the temperature rarely falls below zero degrees. The Hot Spring Pools are popular for residents and visitors alike.

The 25-mile drive from Ouray to Silverton, Colorado, is called the Million Dollar Highway—definitely one of the most spectacular drives in the United States and in the world. The story of how the highway got its name is controversial. Some say the highway cost a million dollars to build; others say there is still a million dollars of gold buried under it.

The area is surrounded by the beautiful San Juan Mountain Range. This stretch of highway rightfully got named "little Switzerland."

We went to Maggie's Kitchen in the Timber Ridge Campground for the most delicious breakfast in Ouray, or so we were told. And it was indeed tasty.

Silverton, Colorado

Silverton is a small town where the famous Silverton-Durango Railroad makes its turn. We boarded the train in Durango and went to Silverton, but we could have boarded in Silverton also. We enjoyed the round trip ride. The famous hotel of the late 1800s, The Grand Imperial Hotel in Silverton, still stands. It is a slice of the past, complete with a long ornate bar with the standard nude above, an upscale gift shop, and a wonderful dining room.

Durango, Colorado

The Silverton-Durango Railroad narrow gauge ride was spectacular beyond description. No wonder it is so famous.

The train itself was built in the late 1800s to carry coal from the mines and was also established as a passenger train. People come from all over the world to experience this ride through the San Juan Mountains of Colorado.

We caught the 9:00 a.m. train out of Durango, though there are lots of times available. The cost is $60.00 a person and includes a two-hour stop in Silverton for lunch and shopping. We got back on the train at 2:45 p.m. and arrived back in Durango about 6:15 p.m.—a full day of "riding the rails."

On this train ride, you can choose assigned seats from either closed cars or open cars. We were told we would see more by riding in the open cars, and that advice was correct. The fall colors in September is an extra treat. (You can make reservations by calling 877-259-5791.)

Tip: If you ride the rails in the open car on the train, be sure to dress in layers. We were not prepared for the changeable Colorado weather. By the time we reached Silverton, I was half frozen. After eating a warm lunch, I headed for a store to purchase some warm clothes. The blanket, gloves, hat, and warm socks made the return trip much more comfortable.

Mesa Verde National Park

Just 36 miles west of Durango is Mesa Verde, a National Park and the location where the Anasazi Indians lived more than a thousand years ago. The cliff dwellings, the museum, the whole area is magnificent. The cliff dwellings at Mesa Verde are ancient multistoried dwellings that fill the cliff-rock alcoves that rise 2,000 feet above the Montezuma Valley. They are unique for their number and remarkable preservation. The cliff dwellings cluster in sandstone canyons. Archaeologists have located more than 4,000 prehistoric sites dating from 550 to 1270 AD.

The sites document the dramatic changes in the lives of a prehistoric people, once dubbed the Anasazi and now more accurately called Puebloans. Forty pueblos and cliff dwellings are visible from park roads and overlooks. Many are open to the public.

The cliff dwellings were discovered in 1888 by two cowboys. Why the Mesa Verde people abandoned their homes may never be known. They left by the end of 13th century. One possible explanation is the very long periods of droughts at that time. Due to repeated years of failed crops, they had to move on to more fertile lands.

The Indians had created a sanctuary for themselves and the place felt very spiritual. They lived off the land and thrived for many hundreds of years, then disappeared. Plan to spend a whole day to experience this place to the fullest.

The closest full service campground to the Park is A & A Mesa Verde Park and Campground. It is open all year. Call 1-800-972-6620 or www.mesaverdecamping.com.

Chama, New Mexico

Another narrow gauge railroad ride is the Cumbres-Tultec Scenic Railroad. We caught this train in Chama, New Mexico. Chama is a small one-street town that caters to train passengers. The 64-mile ride goes from Chama to Antonito, Colorado, with a stop in Osier. The Cumbres-Toltec Scenic Railroad was once the Denver and Rio Grande Western Railroad.

Today, the Cumbres and Toltec Scenic Railroad is America's longest and highest narrow gauge railroad. Narrow gauge means there is only three feet between the rails. This measurement was chosen instead of the more common standard gauges four feet eight inches so that the railroad could make tighter turns in the mountains and thereby reduce construction costs.

We boarded the train and it left promptly at 10:00 a.m. It made several stops where passengers can get off. Some people take the train one-way and ride a bus back. The train returned about 4:20 p.m. We chose to go to Osier where we stopped for lunch and then returned to Chama.

The Cumbres-Toltec Railroad is definitely worth the trip. It gives yet another view of the San Juan Mountains and the vibrant fall colors of late September were awesome. God has painted a beautiful landscape. I hope you will have the opportunity to see it first-hand.

Meeting fun people is part of the great journey we have chosen. At lunch in Osier, we met Esther and Bob Thaller from Los Angeles. We traded names, numbers, and e-mail addresses. I know we will meet again and stay in touch. They have been on the road with their motor home for several months. We knew quickly we had much in common.

San Luis, Colorado

San Luis is a small town in South Central Colorado. A famous artist and talented sculptor Huberto Maestras lives there with his wife Dana and their family. His foundry as well as their gallery is in San Luis.

Huberto was commissioned to do the "Stations of The Cross" in bronze. The stations are placed on a path of about one half mile long leading to a wonderful church at the top of the hill. It is a very spiritual and beautiful place. I thought the sculpture of the "Resurrection" was especially moving. I will always remember the detail and expressions on the faces.

Huberto has his work on display at the Vatican Museum in Rome, Italy. He and his wife are fun people. Do stop in San Luis to see the Stations of the Cross and visit with Huberto and Dana in their gallery.

Heading Home to St. Louis

We had spent five full months in Colorado so we decided it was time to head home to St. Louis. On the way east, we stopped in Bartlesville, Oklahoma, to visit our dear friends Bill and Shirley Foster. In Bartlesville, everything is only about a five-minute drive to anything, or so Bill says. We played 18 holes of golf at an inexpensive course. It was $23.00 for two people and a cart. We also enjoyed a wonderful Corp of Engineers Park that has a beautiful lake. It gave us a chance to launch our boat, The Sea Eagle. The Park also has hook-ups for camping.

We would be in St. Louis for at least a month visiting family and friends and staying at The Casino Queen RV Park. Then we would be "on the road again."

And you could be, too!

Three years ago when I made the decision to Run Away From Home, I definitely had my doubts. Having lived in a familiar place in the

same city all my life had given me security and familiarity that was very comfortable.

I have had to make hard decisions when crises have been thrown into my life. But now, by choice, I was tossing all of my security and comfort away. I often thought, "What am I doing, and why?" In fact, I asked myself this question almost every day.

I kept saying to myself, "Don't look back at what was; look forward at what is to be. If you don't take a chance, you will never know what is out there—all the possibilities of things to do and see."

I love my husband Paul very much. I know that my love for him gave me the courage it took to move forward with this project. I also have a strong belief in God and I put my trust in Him for guidance.

It wasn't easy but a lot of things aren't. I think everything is in one's attitude. I am a strong person having had my strength tested too many times. My strength, my love, my determination helped make this a reality. Looking back at the last three years, I am so grateful we ran away. Life is a kick. My motto: "Live in the Moment and Make Every Day Count." If that's what Running Away also means to you, by all means, DO IT!

Organizations to Join

Escapees RV Club: Call toll free 1-888-757-2582 or 936-327-8873 (Livingston, Texas) or log on to www.escapees.com

AAA (American Automobile Association): 1-800-222-4357. Membership can be obtained in any state. Just call Information in your city.

Coast To Coast: Call toll-free 1-800-368-5721, or log on to www.coastresorts.com

Coast to Coast Deluxe: Call toll-free 1-800-932-6797. Memberships can be purchased in publications as *Trailer Life* or *Family Motor Coach* or log on to www.coastresort.com

Family Motor Coach Association: Call toll free 1-800-543-3622 or log on to www.FMCA.com

Holiday Rambler RV Club: (HRRVC) Call 1-877-702-5415 or email to hrclub@monacohr.com

Western Horizons: Corporate Office, Gunnison, Colorado. Call 970-641-5387.

Passport America: Call toll free 1-800-283-7183.

The Good Sam Club: You can join this club at the participating Good Sam's parks. You will get a 10% discount off the cost of the campground. Call toll free 1-800-234-3450 or log onto www.goodsamclub.com

KOA (Kampgrounds of America): You can join this club at the participating KOA campgrounds. You will get a 10% discount off the cost of the campground. Call the corporate offices at 1-406-248-7444 or log on to www.koa.com

Elderhostel: Call toll free 1-877-426-8056 or log on to www.elderhostel.org

Recommended Books

The *Woodalls* series is a MUST for campers. 847-362-6700 or 1-800-323-9076. Available at many RV dealers or Campers World or log on to: www.woodalls.com

Members can get maps of various areas through AAA (American Automobile Association). A North America Road Atlas can be purchased there also. Log on to www.aaa.com/travel

Helpful Resources

Discounts: Golden Age Passport—Must be purchased at National Parks and Corp of Engineer Parks. The pass entitles two people to camp in National Parks and Corp of Engineer Parks for half price. Admission to the parks is free. Cost is $10.00 for life. For details, log on to www.nps.gov

Insurance: RV Alliance America—Call toll free 1-800-521-2942 or log on to www.rvaa.com

Mail Service: Escapees—Call toll free 1-800-231-9896, 888-757-2582, or in Livingston, Texas, at 936-327-8873. Can also register online at www.escapees.com

Maintenance and Repair: REC TEC RV & Trailer Services, St. Louis, MO 314-731-9080

Sea Eagle Boat: Sea Eagle U.S.A., Division of Hoge Industries, Inc. Port Jefferson, N.Y. 11777: 1-800-852-0925 or log on at www.seaeagle.com

About The Author

Anita Sokolik Henehan was born in St. Louis, Missouri and had lived there all of her life...until recently.

Anita and her first husband Herb Sokolik raised their three children there before a boating accident left her a widow. At the age of 50, this homemaker began a career as an art dealer. She started her art consulting firm called Reflections In Design and began providing art to many large corporations in the U.S. and abroad. After 17 years of operating her business, she sold it to Color Art but remains actively involved.

In May 2000, Anita and her second husband Paul faced their fears, sold their home and belongings, and set out on the road. They have been traveling around North America in their 42-foot motor coach Merrily We Roll Along Two ever since.

In this informative book, she shows other "over-50s" how to overcome their fears and joyfully "run away from home." While she is happily rolling along, she's writing a second book for travelers.

Anita can be reached at 314-308-3785 or via e-mail at henehanmerrily@aol.com

Quick Order Form

Reflections Publishing
4218 Olive Street, St. Louis, MO 63108

How to Run Away from Home After 50
By Anita S. Henehan

Three quick ways to order this book:

1. Telephone: 636-448-5262
2 Clip and mail form to the above address
3. E-mail: henehanmerrily@aol.com

Pricing:

1 book	$14.00 plus $2.50 shipping and handling
6-11 books	$9.80 per book plus $1.25 each shipping
12+ books	$8.40 per book plus $1.25 each shipping

Missouri residents add 7.62% sales tax
Canadian residents: $21.00 CAN each plus shipping

Quantity	Item	Cost	Amount Due
_____	How To Run Away From Home	_____	_____
	ISBN 0-9727951-0-3		
	Shipping and Handling		_____
	Sales tax for Missouri residents 7.62%		_____
		TOTAL	_____

Books will be mailed via Media Mail.

Payment: MC/VISA # _____ Exp._____

Signature _____

Make checks payable to Anita S. Henehan.

Name_____

Address _____

City _____ State _____ Zip _____

Phone _____

Email _____